We the People

THE CITIZEN & THE CONSTITUTION

WE THE PEOPLE
THE CITIZEN & THE CONSTITUTION

LEVEL 1

Center for Civic Education

5115 Douglas Fir Road, Suite J
Calabasas, CA 91302
www.civiced.org
818.591.9321

We the People: The Citizen & the Constitution
Level 1

Directed by the
Center for Civic Education

The contents of this textbook were developed in part under a grant from the U.S. Department of Education. However, those contents do not necessarily represent the policy of the Department of Education, and you should not assume endorsement by the Federal Government.

Cover: Detail from *Washington Crossing the Delaware* by Emanuel Leutze, 1851, The Metropolitan Museum of Art, Gift of John Stewart Kennedy, 1897, Accession Number 97.34, www.metmuseum.org

First Print Edition 1988
Second Print Edition 2003
Third Print Edition 2011
Fourth Print Edition 2020
25 24 23 03 04 05

ISBN-10: 0-89818-222-0

ISBN-13: 978-0-89818-222-4

About We the People: The Citizen and the Constitution

We the People: The Citizen and the Constitution, was developed in 1987 and adopted by the Commission on the Bicentennial of the U.S. Constitution, chaired by Chief Justice Warren E. Burger, as the principal education program of the federal Constitution's bicentennial. The success of the program at the Bicentennial Commission led to Congress continuing the program through the U.S. Department of Education from 1993 to 2011 as an authorized program of the Elementary and Secondary Education Act.

The foundation of the We the People program is the classroom curriculum. It complements the regular school curriculum by providing upper elementary, middle, and high school students with an innovative course of instruction on the history and principles of U.S. constitutional democracy.

The We the People program's culminating activity is a simulated congressional hearing in which students "testify" before a panel of judges acting as members of Congress. Students demonstrate their knowledge and understanding of constitutional principles and have opportunities to evaluate, take, and defend positions on relevant historical and contemporary issues. Teachers may engage their students in a noncompetitive simulated congressional hearing or a competitive hearing at some levels in certain states.

National Advisory Committee

Board of Directors

Acknowledgments

The following staff and consultants contributed to the development of this fourth edition of We the People: The Citizen & the Constitution, *Level 1:*

Principal Writers
Charles N. Quigley
Maria Gallo

Additional Contributors
Margaret Branson
Alissa Irion-Groth
Robert Leming
Mark Molli

Director of Publishing and Digital Content
Mark Gage

Design
Natalia Naduris-Weissman

Editorial Assistant
Megan DeMint

Director of Information Technology
Greg Synnott

Administrative Assistance
Janel Huber
Valerie Milianni

The following staff and consultants contributed to the development of the text upon which the fourth edition is based:

Principal Writers
Charles N. Quigley
Ken Rodriguez

Contributing Writer
Sandra Baker

Illustrator
Richard Stein

Warren E. Burger (1907–1995)

Chief Justice of the United States, 1969–1986

Chair, Commission on the Bicentennial of the United States Constitution

In 1987 Chief Justice of the U.S. Supreme Court Warren E. Burger was the chairman of the Commission on the Bicentennial of the United States Constitution. He wrote these words, which were included in the first edition of this textbook.

The years 1987 to 1991 marked the 200th anniversary of the writing, ratification, and implementation of the basic documents of American democracy, the Constitution and the Bill of Rights. Our Constitution has stood the tests and stresses of time, wars, and change. Although it is not perfect, as Benjamin Franklin and many others recognized, it has lasted because it was carefully crafted by men who understood the importance of a system of government sufficiently strong to meet the challenges of the day, yet sufficiently flexible to accommodate and adapt to new political, economic, and social conditions.

Many Americans have but a slight understanding of the Constitution, the Bill of Rights, and the later amendments to which we pledge our allegiance. The lessons in this book are designed to give you, the next generation of American citizens, an understanding of the background, creation, and subsequent history of the unique system of government brought into being by our Constitution. At the same time, it will help you understand the principles and ideals that underlie and give meaning to the Constitution, a system of government by those governed.

Contents

Contents

Introduction

What Is the Constitution?

The United States Constitution is a written plan that says what our government should do. It also says how our government is to be organized and run.

The Constitution describes what members of our government may do. It also says what they may not do. The Constitution helps prevent the government from violating our rights. Our Constitution is the highest or supreme law of our land. Even the president, Congress, and the Supreme Court must obey the Constitution. In our country, everyone must obey the law.

Our Constitution was written in Philadelphia more than two hundred years ago. We need to understand our Constitution to know our rights and responsibilities as citizens.

This book is not like most history books. Most history books tell the story of people and events of the past. This book is a history of ideas. It explains the most important ideas of our Constitution and tells you how they were developed.

This book will help you understand some of the basic ideals, or goals, of our nation. These ideals include the belief in liberty and justice for all people. You also will learn about your responsibilities as a citizen to help make these ideals a reality for everyone.

The title of each lesson asks an important question about government. After you have finished the lesson, you should be able to answer the question. The answers to the questions will help you understand why the Constitution is important for you.

Your Constitution protects your rights. Here are some of the rights it protects. And here are some of the responsibilities that come along with those rights:

- You have the right to believe in any religion you like. And you are free not to believe in a religion. You are responsible for respecting other people's right to believe what they wish.
- You have the right to tell others your beliefs and ideas. You are responsible for not saying things that could result in serious harm to other people or damage to their property.
- You have the right to the same opportunity others have to do something you want to do. You are responsible for respecting the same right for other people.
- If you are accused of breaking a law, you have the right to be treated fairly. You are responsible for not breaking laws.
- You have the right to ask your government to do things to make things better. You also have the responsibility to not ask for things that are unreasonable and unfair.
- When you are eighteen, you will have the right to vote for people to represent you in your government. You have the responsibility to vote for people who are reasonable and fair.
- When you are an adult, you will have the right to try to get people to elect you to be in government. You have a responsibility to be reasonable and fair when you tell people why they should vote for you.

THE
DECLARATION OF INDEPENDENCE
THE
CONSTITUTION
OF THE
UNITED STATES OF AMERICA
AND THE
BILL OF RIGHTS

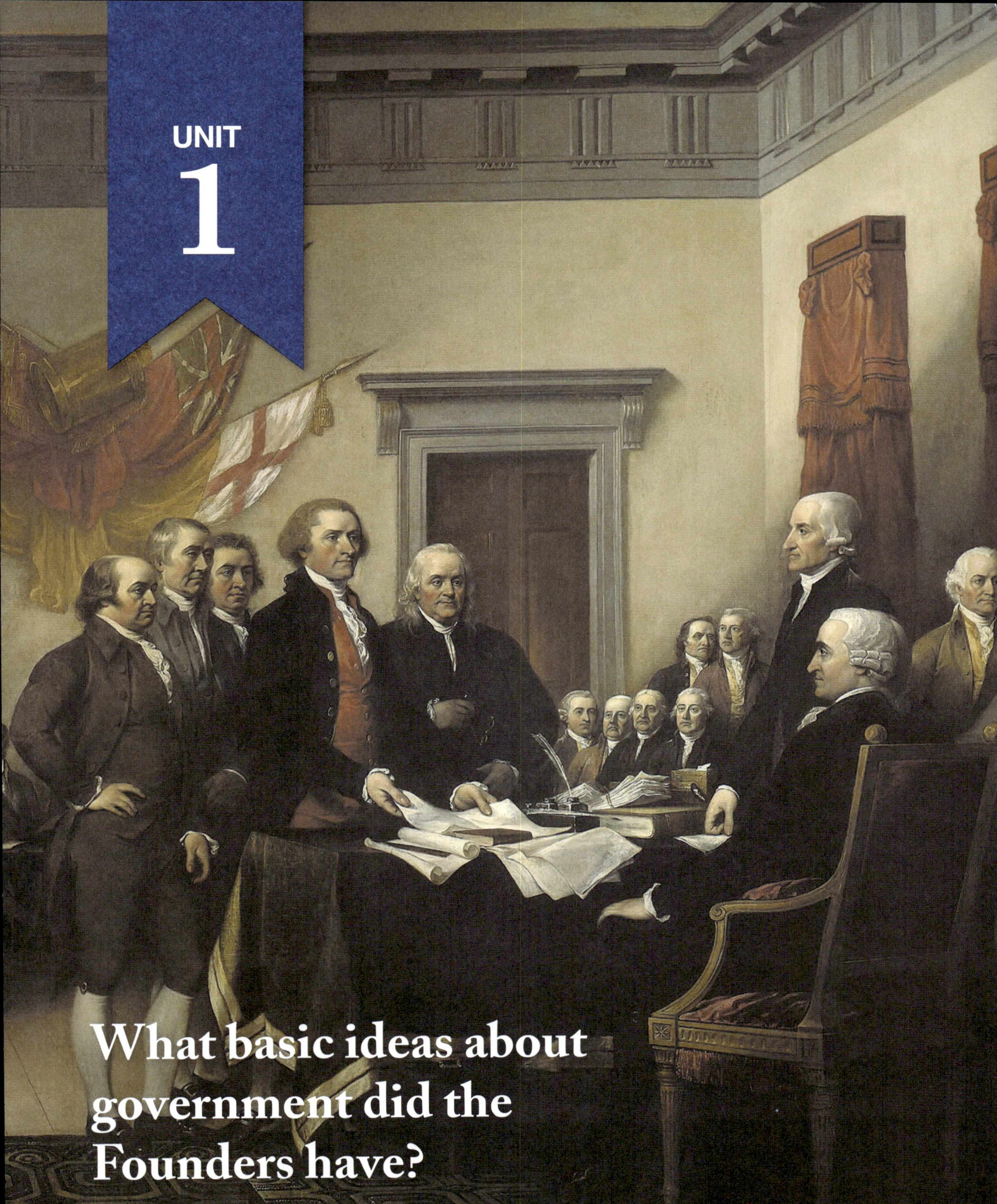

UNIT 1

What basic ideas about government did the Founders have?

UNIT 1

What basic ideas about government did the Founders have?

To understand the United States Constitution, we need to know about the people who wrote it. How did they live? What experiences did they have? What were their ideas about good government?

Your country began more than four hundred years ago. It began as a part of another country called England. England was one of the most powerful countries in the world at that time. It had a large and strong navy with ships that sailed to many parts of the world. Its rulers were called kings or queens. English kings and queens sent people from England and other countries to create new communities in what are now the eastern states of your country. These communities were called colonies. When England united with Scotland, it became known as Great Britain. The colonies became British colonies.

In this unit, we will study their history and their basic ideas about good government.

Studying this unit will help you understand other lessons in this book. More importantly, it will help you understand the basic principles of our government. It will help you understand why our government works the way it does.

KEY TOPICS

- civic virtue
- common good
- consent of the governed
- constitution
- constitutional government
- Declaration of Independence
- natural rights
- purpose of government
- republican government

LESSON

1

What were people like in the British colonies in America during the 1770s?

LESSON PURPOSE

More than two hundred years ago, there were British, Dutch, French, and Spanish colonies in North America. In this lesson, you will learn how people lived in the British colonies. We want to learn about these colonies because they became the United States of America. They were the first thirteen states. This lesson will help you know about the people who wrote our United States Constitution.

LESSON OBJECTIVES

When you have finished this lesson, you should be able to

- ❑ describe what life was like for the average American living in the colonies
- ❑ explain how living in the colonies influenced people's ideas about government, and
- ❑ explain what the term *Founders* means.

TERMS TO KNOW

- colony
- diverse
- Founders
- indentured servant
- plantation
- self-sufficient
- slave
- subject

Who ruled the thirteen colonies?

In the year 1770, our country did not exist. There was no United States of America. The people who were to create our country lived in thirteen British colonies. A **colony** is a territory ruled by another country.

The colonists were subjects of Great Britain. Being a **subject** means that you are under the authority of a government. Great Britain owned and ruled the colonies. The British colonies were on the Atlantic coast of North America. Great Britain was across the ocean more than three thousand miles away.

What was it like to live in the colonies in the 1770s?

When people came from Europe to America, they saw that America was different from where they had lived before. America was a very large place compared to most nations in Europe. There was a great deal of open, unsettled space. The British colonies spread from what is now the state of Maine in the north to Georgia in the south.

There was space in America for people to settle and to own land. In Europe, only the rich could afford to buy land. In the colonies, land was cheap. People came with the hope of owning their own land. Owning land meant that you could farm to support your family. The number of people who

How is this old map of America different from a current map of the United States?

lived in the colonies grew quickly. In 1775, there were 2.5 million people. Fifteen years later, there were almost 4 million people.

Who lived in the colonies?

Because many settlers came to the colonies from Great Britain, they spoke English. They dressed like the British. They followed many of the British customs.

Some colonists were not like the British. They came from many other countries, such as France, Germany, Holland, and Sweden. Each group of settlers brought with them their own customs and ways of life.

Native Americans and their ancestors had lived on the land for thousands of years before the colonists arrived. They had their own customs and ways of life. The settlers called these people Indians. Some Native Americans accepted the settlers and lived peacefully with them. Others fought the settlers. After many battles, some Native Americans were moved from their land by force. Moving Native Americans from their land continued for the next hundred years.

Half a million African people and their descendants also lived in the colonies. They were 20 percent of the population. Most of these people had been brought from Africa to work as slaves. A **slave** is a person who is forced to work without pay and who is not allowed to have any rights.

How was society in the American colonies different from society in Europe?

The colonists treated the slaves as if they were property. Most of the enslaved people were in the Southern Colonies, but slavery existed in all thirteen colonies.

The colonies became home for people from many places and backgrounds. The people brought with them diverse ideas. **Diverse** means to be unlike one another. People held diverse ideas about religion, government, and rights. This diversity helped create a society that was different from society in Europe.

How did the colonists live?

Most Americans in the 1770s were farmers, but not all farms were alike. In the New England Colonies, the cold climate made farming more difficult.

A farm might be only a small fifty-acre patch of rocky soil. On such a farm, family members did all the work themselves. Sometimes they hired a person to help them. Some farmers had an indentured servant. An **indentured servant** was a person who exchanged his or her

What do you think life was like on a small Northern farm? How was life on a large Southern plantation different?

work for a number of years to pay for the trip from Europe to the colonies.

In the Middle Colonies, the soil was good for growing wheat, oats, and barley. People in the Middle Colonies also raised cows, hogs, sheep, and horses. The Middle Colonies had deep rivers. The farmers used the rivers to ship their goods to market.

In the Southern Colonies, the warmer climate made farming easier. Most of the people lived on small farms much like the people in New England. Some people lived on plantations. A **plantation** is a large farm that needs many workers. The slaves and other workers lived on the plantations. Some plantations had hundreds of slaves.

In the 1770s, most Americans were self-sufficient. **Self-sufficient** means that people raised their own food and wove their own cloth for clothes. They built homes and barns, made their own furniture and tools, and even made their own medicines. They traded any extra farm products at a local store for those few goods they could not make for themselves.

What opportunities did people have in America?

A visitor to the colonies would have been impressed by how well the people lived. They lived better than most people anywhere else in the world. There was plenty of work for everyone. The colonists worked hard, but the land was fertile and they grew plenty of food. So most colonists ate better, grew taller, and were healthier than people in Europe.

More people in the colonies could read and write than in any other nation in the world. Many owned enough property to be able to vote. More people had the right to vote than anywhere else in the world. Most of the people had a chance to earn a good living through hard work. Wealth and family name did not mean as much in the colonies as they did in Europe.

However, not all people had the same opportunities. While some people became wealthy, some remained poor. Only adult white men who owned property could vote. In most of the colonies, women were not allowed to own property. In the few cases where women did own property, they were not allowed to vote. Slaves did not have any rights.

Despite these limits, most colonists had more rights than did people in Europe. For example, the colonists could follow their religious beliefs freely. Their rights were very important to them. By 1775, the colonists worried about how to protect their rights.

How are the opportunities that the colonists sought in America in the 1770s different from those that people seek today?

What Do You Think?

What opportunities did this colonial farmer enjoy?

One farmer who wrote about his life in the colonies was Philip Taylor. Read what he wrote. Work with a partner to answer the questions that follow. Be prepared to share your ideas with the class.

> We now have a comfortable dwelling. We have two acres of land planted with potatoes, corn, and melons. I have two hogs, one ewe and her lamb. The price of cows in the spring was as high as 33 dollars. No doubt, I shall have one by fall.
>
> I am living in God's noble and free soil, neither am I slave to others.… I have now been on American soil for two and one-half years and I have not been compelled to pay for the privilege of living. Neither is my cap worn out from lifting it in the presence of gentlemen.

1. What did Philip Taylor like about life in America?
2. What rights did he enjoy?
3. Do you think he would favor a law that does not permit people to buy or sell what they choose? Why?
4. Do you think he would favor a law that gives people more rights because they are wealthy? Why?
5. Do you think he would favor a law that gives people rights because of their family or the group to which they belong? Why?
6. What did he mean when he said, "Neither is my cap worn out from lifting it in the presence of gentlemen"?

Who governed the colonies?

American colonies were ruled by Great Britain from 1607 to 1776, more than one hundred fifty years. George III was king of Great Britain from 1760 to 1820. During much of this time, Great Britain was busy with problems in Europe. The British government did not pay much attention to the colonies. The American colonies learned to govern themselves. They had brought British customs and laws with them to America. They used these British ideas to develop their own governments. The colonists participated in their governments much more than people did in Europe.

During the 1770s, Americans thought about what kind of government they wanted. The colonists asked themselves if King George III was really protecting their rights. There were many arguments, speeches, and books about what was best for the colonies. If you had lived in America then, you would have found it an exciting time.

Who were the Founders?

There were many important leaders in early America. For example, George Washington, Patrick Henry, Abigail Adams, and Benjamin Franklin were all well known during this time. You probably have heard of these people. We call these leaders the **Founders** because they helped found, or establish, our country.

Abigail Adams, one of our nation's Founders and wife of John Adams, wrote to her husband in 1776, "If particular care and attention is not paid to the ladies, we are determined to foment a rebellion, and will not hold ourselves bound by any laws in which we have no voice or representation." What do you think she was concerned about?

The Founders led the fight to free our country from British rule. They developed their own ideas about what type of government would be best for America. The next lessons will help you understand the ideas the Founders used to create our government.

Reviewing and Using the Lesson

1. What was life like for the average American colonist?
2. Why did so many Europeans want to come to live in the colonies?
3. How might living in the colonies help to influence people's ideas about government?
4. What is the meaning of the term *Founders*?

Activities

1. Write a short story about how the colonists' American way of life might have influenced their ideas about government. Share your story with the class.
2. Go to your library or use your computer. Find information about one of the following topics:
   - What was life like for children in the colonies?
   - What was life like for Native Americans in the colonies?
   - What was life like for women in the colonies?
   - What was life like for slaves in the Southern Colonies?
   - What was life like for indentured servants?

   Share what you learned with your class.
3. Find a map of the United States today. Locate the original thirteen colonies. What were the names of the thirteen colonies? Which ones were New England Colonies, Middle Colonies, and Southern Colonies?
4. On a map of the United States, locate your state. Was your state originally a British colony? Was it a French or Spanish colony? What Native American tribes lived there before the Europeans came? When did your state become part of the United States?

LESSON 2

Why did the Founders believe that people needed a government?

LESSON PURPOSE

In this lesson, you will learn some of the Founders' most important ideas about our basic rights. You will learn the Founders' beliefs about where these rights come from. Finally, you will learn why the Founders believed that people must have government.

LESSON OBJECTIVES

When you finish this lesson, you should be able to explain the Founders' ideas about our rights and the purposes of our government.

TERMS TO KNOW

- consent
- consent of the governed
- liberty
- life
- natural rights
- property
- social contract
- state of nature

Critical Thinking Exercise

Before you learn about the Founders' beliefs about rights, let's examine your own ideas about rights. Then you can compare your ideas with theirs. You will probably find that you and the Founders have many of the same ideas.

Do you think you should have the right to believe in any religion you wish? Do you think you should have the right to speak freely?

Work with a partner or in a group of three to five students. Together, answer the questions that follow. Be prepared to share your ideas with the class.

1. List the rights you think you should have. Why do you think it is important to have these rights?

2. Which rights seem most important? Arrange the rights you listed in order. Place the most important first. Why do you think these rights are the most important? What responsibilities come with each of these rights?

3. Do you think people everywhere should have these rights? Why or why not?

What rights do all people have? Why do you think they have these rights?

What natural rights did the Founders believe all people have from the time they are born?

What were the Founders' beliefs about rights?

Most of the Founders believed that people have certain **natural rights**. These included the rights to life, liberty, and property. All persons have natural rights just because they are human beings. Everyone is born with these rights. No one can take these rights away. Here is what these natural rights mean.

- **Life** is the right to live without fear of being injured or killed by others.
- **Liberty** is the right to be free. Some examples of liberties are the rights to believe what you wish, to read what you want, to speak freely, and to travel wherever you want to go.
- **Property** is the right to own things such as books, a house, land, or a business. Your labor or work is also your property.

Do you agree with John Locke's ideas? Why or why not?

What problems might we have protecting our rights?

The Founders knew that protecting the rights of the people was not an easy thing to do. Sometimes people try to take away the rights of others. The Founders thought they should have a plan to protect their own rights and the rights of others.

Many Founders had read a book by John Locke. John Locke was an Englishman. He lived from 1632 to 1704. Locke wrote about natural rights. His ideas help us to understand more clearly the problem of protecting the rights of people.

John Locke suggested that you imagine living in a state of nature. A **state of nature** is a situation where there is no government, no rules, and no laws. Think about what your life might be like in a state of nature.

Critical Thinking Exercise

What might happen if there were no rules, laws, or government?

Imagine that you live on an island far away. There are no rules, no laws, and no government. There is no one to tell you what to do.

Work with a partner or in a group of three to five students.

Together answer the following questions. Be prepared to share your ideas with the class.

1. Would anyone have the right to govern you? Would you have the right to govern anyone else? Why?
2. Would you have any rights? What might they be?
3. What might people who were smarter or stronger than others try to do? Why?
4. What might people who were not as smart as others or who were weaker than others try to do? Why?
5. What might life be like for you, your family, and everyone else in a state of nature?

What would life be like without any government? How would people protect their rights?

What did John Locke say might happen if there were no rules, laws, or government?

You just had a chance to think about your rights in a state of nature. Now, you might want to compare your thinking with that of John Locke. Locke thought that life would be very difficult without laws or government. He worried about the problems that might happen. He said the following:

1. Some people might try to take away other people's rights. The stronger people might force the weaker people to do the things the stronger people want. The weaker people might unite against the stronger people.
2. People would have natural rights, but their rights would not be safe.
3. It would be very hard to live a safe, peaceful, and happy life in a state of nature.

According to John Locke, what might life be like in a state of nature?

How might individuals protect their natural rights in a state of nature?

Why did the Founders believe we needed a government?

John Locke wrote about how to solve the problems of life in a state of nature. He said people could make a social contract. A **social contract** is an agreement among the people to set up a government. The people agree to give up something and then they receive something in return.

The people give up some of their freedom. They **consent**, or agree, to create a government and laws. The **consent of the governed** means that the people consent to obey the laws and the government they create. The people no longer will be able to do whatever they want.

What the people gain is protection for their rights. The government protects the rights of the people. It protects their rights to life, liberty, and property. People would feel safer than they did in a state of nature. The people might live more secure and happier lives.

The Founders believed that people need government to protect their rights. Therefore, the main purpose of government, they said, is to protect a person's rights to life, liberty, and property.

Reviewing and Using the Lesson

1. What basic rights did the Founders believe people should have?
2. What are natural rights? How do you get natural rights?
3. What might life be like if there were no rules, laws, or government?
4. What is a social contract?
5. What did the Founders think should be the main purpose of government?

Activities

1. Write a paragraph explaining what life might be like in a state of nature and why we need government. Draw a cartoon to illustrate your main points.
2. Write a short story that tells how the rights to life, liberty, and property apply to you and your family. Share your story with the class.
3. Go to the library or use your computer to learn more about John Locke and his ideas. Share what you learned with the class.
4. Read the Mayflower Compact. What are the three main things the signers of the compact agreed to do? Explain how the Mayflower Compact is an example of a social contract. Share what you learned with your class.

LESSON
3

What is a republican government?

LESSON PURPOSE

The Founders gained some of their ideas about government from studying history. They used this knowledge when they created our government. They did not create a democracy like we have today. They created a republic.

LESSON OBJECTIVES

When you have finished this lesson, you should be able to explain

- ❑ the difference between a direct democracy and a republic,
- ❑ why the Founders created a republic instead of a democracy,
- ❑ some of the advantages of republican government, and
- ❑ the importance of the concepts of common good and civic virtue.

TERMS TO KNOW

- assembly
- civic virtue
- common good
- direct democracy
- interests
- represent
- representative democracy
- representatives
- republican government
- Roman Republic
- senate

Who ruled the Roman republic?

Where did the Founders get their ideas about government?

The Founders got some of their ideas about government by studying the history of ancient Greece and Rome. They learned that at one time the city of Athens in Greece had a direct democracy. This meant that all of the citizens of Athens had the right to meet to make their own laws. They also had the right to choose their own leaders. However, many of the people who lived in Athens were not citizens. They were slaves or other workers who did not have the same rights as citizens.

The Founders knew about direct democracy from their own experience. Many of their towns had direct democracies where people met together to make laws for themselves.

The Founders also studied the history of the **Roman Republic**. The Roman Republic was not just a city like Athens. It governed a very large country with hundreds of communities. Rome was the capital of the Republic. Today Rome is the capital of Italy.

For some time, the Roman Republic was ruled by a senate and an assembly. The **senate** was made up of representatives chosen by some of the largest, oldest, and richest families of Rome. The **assembly** was made up of representatives of a wealthy middle class of Roman citizens.

The senate and assembly made all of the laws for the Roman Republic. Each year, the senate elected two leaders called consuls. They were responsible for carrying out the laws made by the senate and assembly. There were thousands of slaves and other people who lived in the Republic, but were not citizens and did not have the same rights as citizens.

The Founders learned how citizens of such a large country like the Roman Republic could rule themselves. The Founders used some of the ideas they learned from the Romans to create our government. Let's examine some of these ideas.

How can the people rule themselves?

Direct democracy means that the people themselves decide what laws they need. In many of the American colonies, people lived in small towns. If there was a problem in the community, the leaders called a town meeting. The people of the town came to the meeting. They talked about the problem and decided what was best for their town. A town meeting is a form of direct democracy. As communities grow larger, it becomes harder for everyone to get together to make decisions in town meetings.

In a **representative democracy**, all the people in a country over a certain age, such as eighteen, have the right to elect representatives to make laws for them. They also have the right to try to be elected as a representative

Why would elections be an important part of a republican government?

or other leader in government, such as a president or governor of a state. Elected representatives are responsible for making and carrying out laws that protect everyone's rights and help everyone, not just a few people.

The government of Rome was called a republican government. The Founders read that a **republican government** was one in which

- the power of government was held by representatives of certain groups of citizens, such as in the Roman senate and assembly,
- the citizens give power to leaders they elect to **represent** them and to serve their **interests**, and
- the representatives are responsible for helping all the citizens in the country, not just a few of them.

How did the Founders use some of the ideas from the Roman Republic?

The Founders were influenced by some of the ideas they learned from the Roman Republic when they created our government. They thought it was a good way to govern a large country like the United States. But they changed some of the ideas to make them better for America. The following is how they used those ideas.

- **Representatives are selected to serve the common good.** Representatives do not favor one group of people, such as the rich or the poor. Representatives make laws to help everyone.
- **Having representatives make the laws is more efficient.** In a direct democracy, everyone helps make the laws. Making laws takes time. The people have to study every problem to make good and fair laws. People do not have time. They have to earn a living. Having everyone in a large country make the law raises too many problems. Representatives can make laws faster and better because it is their job.
- **The people have a say in their government.** The people do not give up their voice in government. They decide who will represent them. The people can tell their representatives what they want them to do.
- **The representatives have to listen to the people.** The people expect their representatives to make good and fair laws. If the representatives do not make good and fair laws, the people can vote them out of office. The people can choose new leaders to represent them.

What changes have taken place to bring about more equal representation since the founding of the country?

How did our country change from a republic to a democratic republic?

When our country began, just like in ancient Athens and Rome, only some of the people living in the country were citizens with the right to vote. Women, Native Americans, and slaves were not citizens and not allowed to vote or run for public office. Only white men with a certain amount of property could vote and run for office.

Over more than 150 years of our history, other people struggled to get the same rights as white men with property. Because almost everyone over the age of eighteen now has the right to vote and run for public office, the United States has become a representative democracy, which is also known as a democratic republic.

What is the common good?

One of the most important ideas the Founders learned from the Roman Republic was the "common good." The Romans thought that the main purpose of republican government is to promote the common good. The **common good** means what is best for the community as a whole. When a government tries to help everyone in a country, we say it is serving the common good. The common good is what is good for everyone in the country, not just a few people.

What kinds of citizens make a republican government work well?

When you work to help others and promote the common good, you are showing **civic virtue**. The Founders thought that people must have civic virtue for a republican government to work. People with civic virtue are interested in having their government help all the people.

The Founders felt it was necessary to teach children the importance of helping others. Young people learned about civic virtue in their homes, schools, and churches. Adults also heard about civic virtue from their religious and political leaders.

The Founders thought a republican government would work in the new country. They believed that most of the people had civic virtue. They thought the people would select leaders who would work for the common good.

What are some things you think government could do that would be good for everyone?

Critical Thinking Exercise

How can we decide what is for the common good?

How do you decide what the common good is? When should you give up your own interests to do something that is good for everyone? Each one of us has to answer this question personally. The following exercise will help you do this.

Work with a partner. Discuss the questions. Be prepared to share your ideas with the class.

1. What might be a situation in your school in which you should try to do what is best for everyone?
2. What might be a situation in your school in which you should do something for yourself and not try to help others?
3. People often do not agree about what is best for everyone. Describe a situation in your school where people might disagree. How would you decide what the common good is in this situation?
4. What are some things that leaders in your school should do to promote the common good?

What Do You Think?

Why is civic virtue important?

Read the story of "Cincinnatus, Citizen of Rome." Work in a group of three to five students. Answer the questions that follow the story. Be prepared to share your responses with the class.

Cincinnatus, Citizen of Rome

In the year 460 B.C., Rome was in great danger. The enemy surrounded the army of Rome on all sides. They were burning people's homes and stealing their property.

The leaders of the Roman government called for a meeting. They decided to ask a farmer named Cincinnatus to help them during the crisis. Cincinnatus was a hard worker. He owned four acres of land on which to grow food to feed his family.

Cincinnatus once had been a skilled leader of the army. The government sent messengers to find him. When the messengers arrived, he was quietly plowing the fields. They asked him to serve as ruler of Rome for as long as the crisis might last.

Cincinnatus loved his country. He left his plow to go to Rome to lead the army. In a battle that lasted two days, his army defeated the enemy. Cincinnatus saved the country.

The people of Rome honored and praised Cincinnatus. When the battle was over, he did not try to remain as a ruler of his country. He did not want power and fame. Instead, he returned to his home and his life as a farmer and an ordinary citizen.

What would you have done if you were Cincinnatus? Why?

If Cincinnatus had remained as ruler of Rome, would he have been practicing civic virtue? Why or why not?

1. In the story, what was the common good for the citizens of Rome?
2. What self-interests did Cincinnatus have in this story?
3. Do you think Cincinnatus had civic virtue? Why or why not?
4. Why is it important that citizens in a republican government have civic virtue?
5. Describe someone you know who has civic virtue. What did the person do to cause you to think she or he has civic virtue?

Reviewing and Using the Lesson

1. What is a republican government? How is it different from a direct democracy?
2. What are representatives in a republican government supposed to do?
3. What are the advantages of a republican government?
4. What is the role of citizens in a republican government?
5. Define the term *common good*. Give examples of the common good in your school, community, and country.
6. Define the term *civic virtue*. Why is it important that citizens have civic virtue?

Activities

1. What is a town meeting like? Hold a town meeting in your class to make rules for your classroom. Find a book in your library or use the computer to learn how to conduct a town meeting. Do you think it would be a good idea to hold a town meeting of your whole school to make school rules? Why or why not? Share what you learned with the class.
2. Use a dictionary. What is the difference between republican and Republican? What is the difference between democrat and Democrat? Draw a cartoon that illustrates how the terms are different. Share your work with the class.
3. As a class, write a letter or choose a representative to make a telephone call to a member of your town, city, or tribal council. Ask the council member to explain some things he or she does to promote the common good of your community. Ask if there has been a time when people's self-interest conflicted with what was thought to be the common good. What happened?
4. Make a list of things that students in your classroom can do to promote the common good in your school. What can you do to promote the common good in your neighborhood or community?

LESSON 4

What is a constitutional government?

LESSON PURPOSE

You have learned what the Founders believed about natural rights, the common good, and civic virtue. In this lesson, there are two other important things to study and understand. The first is a constitution, and the other is constitutional government. You will learn to explain the difference between the two.

LESSON OBJECTIVES

When you have finished this lesson, you should be able to explain

- ❑ what you can learn about a nation by studying its constitution,
- ❑ what a constitutional government is, and
- ❑ the difference between a constitutional government and a dictatorial government.

TERMS TO KNOW

- constitution
- constitutional government
- dictatorial government
- limit

Critical Thinking Exercise

Which rules and laws are about government?

Complete this exercise in groups of three to five students. Be prepared to explain your findings to the class.

Read the list of rules and laws. For each rule or law, follow these instructions. Your teacher will give you a chart. On the chart, write the number of each rule or law that explains something about how a government is to be run. Be prepared to explain the rule or law and what it does.

Then, write the number of each rule or law that does not explain something about how a government is to be run.

Rules and laws

1. Congress cannot make any laws that unfairly limit your right to speak freely.
2. Don't speak with your mouth full.
3. Take turns on the swings on the playground.
4. You must finish your assignment before you go out for recess.
5. The president must be elected every four years.
6. Everyone eighteen years old and older has the right to vote.

Why is it important to know how a government is organized and how it works?

What is a constitution?

In the previous exercise, you should have found some rules and laws that explain how a government is to be run. You also should have found some rules that do not have anything to do with how a government should be run.

When you found the rules and laws that tell how a government should be run, you found parts of a constitution. A **constitution** is a set of rules and laws that explain how a government is organized and how it should be run. Most constitutions are written. Some are partly unwritten. Some are not written at all. According to our definition, every nation has a constitution. Fair governments and unfair governments have constitutions.

Studying the constitution of a government will help you answer certain questions about that government and its citizens. Here are some of the questions a constitution usually answers.

Questions about the government

- What are the purposes of the government?
- How is the government organized? What parts does it have? What does each part do?
- How is the government supposed to carry out its business? How are rules made?
- How are people chosen to serve in the government?

Questions about citizens

- Who is a citizen?
- Are citizens supposed to have control over their government? If so, how do they control it?
- What rights and responsibilities, if any, are citizens supposed to have?

What is a constitutional government?

Just because a nation has a constitution does not mean it has a constitutional government. A **constitutional government** means that there are limits on the powers of government. A **limit** is a point beyond which someone or something cannot go. The United States Constitution says there are certain kinds of laws that Congress cannot make. The Constitution does not permit the president to do whatever he or she wants to do. In a constitutional government, the constitution sets limits on what the people who run the government are allowed to do.

It is not enough for a constitution to say what the limits on the powers of government are. The people who run the government must obey the constitution. A constitution also must provide ways to enforce the limits it sets forth. One way is to have regular and free elections. The citizens can vote to remove people from office if they do not obey the constitution.

Why is it important to limit the power of those who run the government?

What is a dictatorial government?

A **dictatorial government** means that there are no limits on the power of the people who run the government. They can do whatever they want to do.

Can you have a constitution and still have a dictatorial government? The answer is yes. A constitution might give a person unlimited power. The constitution might limit power but not have ways to enforce those limits. There might be ways to enforce the limits, but no one actually enforces them.

Critical Thinking Exercise

Why is it important to limit a government's powers?

You have learned that constitutional governments have limits on their powers. Why do we need such limits? The following story might help you understand why. It is based on a section from a book called *Two Years Before the Mast*. Richard Henry Dana (1815–1882), a famous American author, wrote the book.

It is a true story about Dana's experiences. When he was young, he worked on a ship that sailed from New England around South America to the West Coast.

At that time, there were no laws that placed reasonable limits on the powers of a ship's captain. Because of this story and the efforts of other people, laws were passed to limit the powers of captains.

When you have finished reading, work in groups of three to five students to answer the questions at the end of the story.

Life on a sailing ship

The Captain of our ship had been losing his temper frequently. He threatened to whip the cook for throwing food on the deck. He got furious when the mate bragged that he could tie knots better than the Captain could. Most of his anger, however, was directed against Sam.

Sam couldn't speak clearly, and he worked more slowly than the others. Still, he was a good sailor, and he tried to do his best. The Captain just didn't like him.

One Saturday morning, I heard the Captain shouting at someone. Then I heard the noise of a fight.

What would you have done if you were Sam? Why?

"You may as well keep still, for I have got you," said the Captain. "Will you ever talk back to me again?"

"I never did, sir," said Sam.

"That's not what I asked you. Will you ever talk back to me again?"

"I never have," Sam said again.

"Answer my question, or I'll have you whipped!"

"I'm no slave," said Sam.

"Then I'll make you one," said the Captain. He sprang up to the deck and called the mate. "Tie that man up! I'll teach you all who is master of this ship!"

"Why are you going to whip that man, sir?" asked John.

Upon hearing this, the Captain turned to John and ordered him to be put in chains.

Watching this made me sick. I wanted to stop it. There were only a few others who felt as I did. If we tried to free John and Sam, we would lose. Then we would be accused of mutiny. Even if we won, we would have to be pirates for life. If we were ever caught, we would be punished. A sailor has no rights. He has to do what the Captain orders or become a pirate.

The Captain whipped both men without mercy. When John asked why he was being whipped, the Captain answered, "Because you ask questions." Then he whipped him harder and harder.

I was horrified. I couldn't watch any more.

At last the Captain stopped.

He turned to us. "Now you see how things are! Now you know what I am! I'm the slave driver, and you are all my slaves! I'll make you all do as I say, or I'll whip you all!"

Should the powers of a ship's captain be limited? Why?

What procedures should the review board follow when conducting a hearing?

Class Activity

The year is 1840. In the United States there are no laws that set reasonable limits on the power of a ship's captain. A Naval Review Board looks into problems that occur aboard sailing ships. Recently, a new problem came to the board's attention. A young sailor wrote a book. In the book he raises questions about the limits on the power of a ship's captain.

The board members will conduct a hearing. They will listen to the people affected by this problem. Then the Board will decide how to solve the problem.

First, let's look at the job of a ship's captain. Then let's look at what a ship's captain may not do.

A ship's captain has the duty and the power to

1. Supervise the running of the ship
2. Decide what course the ship will sail
3. Assign people on board the ship to do different jobs
4. Settle disagreements among sailors
5. Punish sailors who break rules
6. Write reports to the ship's owners
7. Keep a daily log of the ship's progress

A ship's captain may not

1. Risk the success of the voyage
2. Punish by death sailors who have broken rules

Why does each group have a different opinion about how much power a ship's captain should have?

Getting ready

Your class will work in five groups. Each group should take one of the roles described below. Four groups should prepare to make a presentation to the Naval Review Board. The group should explain its ideas about limiting the power of the ship's captain. They should also prepare to answer questions from the Naval Review Board.

- **Naval Review Board** Select a member of the group to be the president of the board. Study the role of each group. Prepare questions to ask each of the groups who will make a presentation to the board. The questions should help you to understand the position of each of the groups. The responses to the questions should help you reach a decision about what to do about the power of a ship's captain.
- **Captain** Prepare arguments against any changes in the limits on the power of a ship's captain. Explain why the captains do not want their power limited.
- **Crew** Prepare arguments in favor of limiting the power of a ship's captain. Propose specific limits on captains' powers that you would like the board to make.
- **Owners of the ships** Prepare your arguments against limiting the power of a ship's captain.
- **Author and friends** Prepare your arguments in favor of changing the power of the captains.

Taking part

The president of the Naval Review Board will start the meeting. Each group has four minutes to explain its position to the board.

After each presentation, the board members may ask questions of the group. Each person in the group should help answer the questions.

After hearing all the groups, the Naval Review Board will meet and decide what to do.

Talking it over

1. In the story, was the government of the ship more like a constitutional government or a dictatorial government? Why?
2. What were the strongest arguments the ship owners and captains made against limiting a captain's power?
3. What were the strongest arguments the crew and the author made in favor of limiting a captain's power?
4. Do you agree with the decision of the Naval Review Board? Why? Naval Review Board students may explain how they reached their decision.
5. Did the decision of the Naval Review Board help to protect the rights of sailors? If so, how?
6. Why do you think it is important to have a constitutional government?

Why is it important to listen to all sides of an issue?

Reviewing and Using the Lesson

1. What is a constitution?

2. What can you learn about a nation's government by studying its constitution?

3. Why did the Founders think that it is necessary to limit the power of government?

4. How did the Founders think the power of government could be limited?

5. Explain the difference between a constitution and a constitutional government.

6. Explain the differences between a dictatorial government and a constitutional government.

Activities

1. Turn to the Constitution at the back of this book. Read Article I, Section 8. What powers does Congress have? Now read Section 9. What limits on its powers does Congress have?

2. Draw a cartoon or picture that shows the difference between a constitutional government and a dictatorial government.

3. In the history of the world, there have been governments that did not have proper limits on their power. Examples of such governments include Nazi Germany and the former Soviet Union. Find information about these governments. What are some examples of how these governments violated the natural rights of the people? Share what you learned with the class.

LESSON 5

What ideas did the Founders use in the Declaration of Independence?

LESSON PURPOSE

In 1776, the American colonies broke away from British rule. They chose to be a free country. The Founders wrote a special statement to explain why they wanted to be independent. This statement is called the Declaration of Independence.

The Declaration of Independence is one of the most important writings in American history. It describes the major ideas the Founders had about government. The Declaration also lists the Founders' complaints against the British king.

LESSON OBJECTIVES

When you have finished this lesson, you should be able to explain some of the main ideas in the Declaration of Independence. As you will see, they are ideas you have already studied and discussed.

TERMS TO KNOW

- American Revolution
- Declaration of Independence
- First Continental Congress
- Loyalists
- Patriots
- principle
- Second Continental Congress

What does this picture show about the way the British government treated the colonies at first?

What problems did the colonists have with the British government?

For many years, the British government let the colonists govern themselves. Britain was busy fighting wars with other European countries. In the 1760s, however, Britain began to tighten its control. The British government passed new laws taxing the colonists and controlling their trade. The colonists became alarmed. They felt their rights were not being protected. The colonists did not have the right to vote for people to represent them in the British government. Some argued that the British government had no right to tax them. They said, "No taxation without representation!"

Great Britain felt it had the right to tax the colonies and control their trade. People in Britain were paying high taxes to support and defend the American colonies. They thought the colonists should pay their fair share of taxes since they received the benefits of being a part of Great Britain. Many Americans became angry about the new trade laws and taxes.

What prompted the American Revolution?

In 1774, twelve colonies sent representatives to a meeting in Philadelphia. This meeting was called the **First Continental Congress**. Congress tried to find ways to get the British to change the laws. It sent a protest to the British government. Congress then ordered that the buying and selling of British goods be stopped. It also began to organize a citizens' army. Soon there was talk of fighting the British.

In April 1775, the British sent soldiers to look for some colonists who they thought were rebels. When the sides met near Boston, they began shooting at each other. War between Britain and the American colonies had begun. The **American Revolution** was underway, but the colonists had not yet declared their independence.

How did Great Britain's control of the colonies change in the 1760s?

What caused the colonies to declare their independence from Great Britain?

Why did the Founders write the Declaration of Independence?

The colonists sent delegates to the **Second Continental Congress** after the first incident of the Revolution. They were still thinking about ways to get Britain to change its policies. Soon, however, they were conducting the war.

In the spring of 1776, more and more colonists were in favor of independence. Congress wanted to wait until all the states agreed before it declared independence. In the meantime, Congress appointed a committee to write a declaration.

The declaration would explain to the world why the colonists were declaring independence and why they had a right to do so. The committee asked one of their members, Thomas Jefferson, to write the declaration. Jefferson was known to be an excellent writer. The **Declaration of Independence** that he wrote describes the basic principles of the new nation. A **principle** is a rule or belief about how to behave. Congress voted to accept the Declaration on July 4, 1776.

What ideas about government are in the Declaration of Independence?

In writing the Declaration, the Founders used some of the main ideas you have studied to explain why they wanted to be free from Great Britain. The Declaration of Independence has three parts:

1. Basic ideas about people and government
2. Reasons why the Founders thought they had the right to be free from British rule
3. Complaints against the British king

These parts of the Declaration are so important that it is worth learning more about them.

1. Basic ideas about people and government

These include the idea that all people are "created equal." They are born with certain rights that no one can take away. Among these rights are rights to "life, liberty, and the pursuit of happiness." The purpose of government is to protect these rights.

2. Reasons why the Founders thought they had the right to be free from British rule

The Declaration also says that the power of government comes from the consent of the people. People are the masters of government and not the other way around. If a government violates the rights of its people, the people can change the government or get rid of it and create a new one.

What did the Founders think about the role of government?

3. Complaints against the British king

To prove that the king had violated their rights, the Founders included a long list of complaints against him. The complaints are based on the idea that government should protect the rights of the people and serve the common good.

- He refused to approve laws made by the colonists that were necessary for their common good.
- He closed the colonists' legislatures when they opposed his violation of the rights of the people.
- He kept a standing army in the colonies even though there was no war.
- He stopped the colonists' trade with other countries.
- He taxed the colonists without their consent.
- He took away the colonists' right to a trial by jury.

Why did some colonists reject the idea of independence?

John Adams was one of the Founders who strongly supported the Declaration of Independence. He said that not everyone wanted the colonies to become independent from Great Britain. At the time the Declaration was written, he said that about one-third of the colonists wanted independence. They were called the **Patriots**. They agreed with the ideas and arguments in the Declaration of Independence.

Adams said that about one-third of the colonists had not made up their minds about independence. Finally, about one-third of the colonists did not want to become independent. They were called **Loyalists** because they believed the colonies should stay loyal or faithful to the king.

Many Loyalists were large landowners or wealthy merchants. They thought their businesses would be hurt. Other Loyalists had been appointed to their jobs by the king. If the colonies became independent, they would lose their jobs. Even if the Loyalists did not like British taxes and other limits on their freedom, they did not think that breaking with Great Britain was the way to solve those problems.

Many Loyalists joined the British army and fought for the king. Some Loyalists moved back to Great Britain. Others went to Canada or to the West Indies. Those who stayed in the colonies had a hard time. Sometimes their property was taken from them. Some Loyalists were treated cruelly or put in jail.

What happened to some Loyalists who angered the colonists?

What Do You Think?

Why should you support the idea of independence?

Imagine that you are a Patriot. You want to convince everybody that they should support the idea of independence from Great Britain. You have some friends and neighbors who are Loyalists and some who do not want to choose sides.

Work in groups of two to three students to write a letter to the newspaper in your colony. Explain why the colonies should become independent. Use the ideas, reasons for independence, and complaints stated in the Declaration of Independence.

What were some reasons for the colonies to stay loyal to Great Britain?

What were some reasons for the colonies to become independent?

Reviewing and Using the Lesson

1. Why did the Founders feel that the British government was not protecting their rights?
2. Why did the Founders write the Declaration of Independence?
3. According to the Declaration of Independence, why do people set up a government?
4. According to the Declaration of Independence, how do governments get their power?
5. According to the Declaration of Independence, what action may the people take if government does not protect their rights? How is this right related to the idea of consent of the governed?
6. Why did some people in the colonies not support the Declaration of Independence?
7. How important are the ideals of the Declaration of Independence to you today? Why?

Activities

1. Some laws that the British passed were the Tea Act of 1773, the Quartering Act, and the Coercive Acts. Learn more about these laws. Write a speech explaining either why these laws violated the rights of the colonists or why they were necessary.
2. Women played an important part in the Revolutionary War. Choose one of these women. Write a report about her accomplishments for your class.
    - Abigail Adams
    - Lydia Darragh
    - Nancy Hart
    - Sybil Ludington
    - Mercy Otis Warren
    - Molly Pitcher
    - Deborah Samson
    - Phillis Wheatley
    - Elizabeth "Betty" Zane
3. How did Native Americans help the colonists in the Revolutionary War?
4. Find out about African Americans who fought in the Revolutionary War. Which side did they fight for? Explain why. Write a report. Read your report to the class.

LESSON
6

What were the first state governments like?

LESSON PURPOSE

When the American colonies became independent from Great Britain, they needed new governments. Colonial leaders set about writing constitutions for their new states. In this lesson, you will learn about the new state governments.

LESSON OBJECTIVES

When you have finished this lesson, you should be able to explain

- ❑ some important ideas used in the state constitutions and
- ❑ how the state constitutions protected the rights of citizens.

TERMS TO KNOW

- bill of rights
- checks and balances
- executive branch
- higher law
- judicial branch
- legislative branch
- separation of powers

How did the people govern themselves after declaring their independence from Great Britain?

In 1776, British government in the colonies came to an end. The colonies were now free and independent states. They were free to rule themselves. To do so, each state had to set up a new government. A few states wrote constitutions before the Declaration of Independence. Most of the states wrote their constitutions some months later.

At that time, most Americans did not think of themselves as one nation. They were loyal to their states. Some people believed that the states should be united. They needed a way to control trade among the states and with other countries. They also needed a way to manage conflicts that might arise among the states. A national government could help do these things.

A closer look at the state governments the people set up will help us to better understand the United States Constitution. First, we will look at the state governments. In the next lesson, we will look at the national government.

How does this picture illustrate the idea of separation of powers?

What kind of state governments did the people create?

The people in the states put into practice the ideas and beliefs they shared about government. They used the following ideas in their state constitutions. You studied most of them in earlier lessons.

Ideas about natural rights

- The purpose of government is to protect a person's rights to life, liberty, and property.

Ideas about republican government

- All power comes from the people. The people give some of their power to the government. The people elect members of government to represent them.

Ideas about constitutional government

- The constitution limits the power of people in the government.

- The constitution is a **higher law**. This means that lawmakers cannot make laws that violate the constitution. It also means that all people in government must obey the constitution.

- One way to limit power is by **separation of powers**. This means that power is divided among three branches. The three branches are the legislative, the executive, and the judicial.

The state constitutions gave most of the power to the **legislative branch**. It made the laws. The people elected representatives to make the laws. People believed that it was the safest branch in which to place most of the power. It was the branch closest to the people. Therefore, it was most likely to protect the rights of citizens.

The **executive branch** carried out and enforced the laws. The state executive was the governor. People believed that they should not trust the governor with too much power. It was not so easy for the people to control the governor. Once elected, a governor did not need to be close to the people.

The **judicial branch** decided what the laws mean. This branch settled conflicts. It decided what to do with people who did not follow the law. The people did not want to give the judicial branch too much power. They remembered how the king's judges had treated them in the British courts.

The state constitutions also set up a system of **checks and balances**. The three branches checked, or stopped, each other when necessary. In this way, they kept each branch from gaining too much power.

What ideas about rights were included in the state constitutions?

How did the state constitutions protect the rights of citizens?

Most states wrote declarations or bills of rights. A **bill of rights** is a list of the rights of citizens. It was usually the first part of a state's constitution. These are some rights of citizens that most states wrote into their constitutions. The right to

- vote in free and frequent elections,
- freedom of speech and of the press,
- representation on tax matters,
- have a lawyer if accused of a crime,
- trial by jury,
- protection from illegal search and seizure, and
- protection from cruel and unusual punishment.

Some state constitutions did not allow the state to keep a militia in time of peace. A militia is a group of citizens who receive military training. Most of the state constitutions also did not allow the state to force people to let soldiers live in their houses.

What Do You Think?

What did the Massachusetts Constitution say about education?

The Massachusetts Constitution was adopted in 1780. Many people think it was the best of the state constitutions. Ideas found in the Massachusetts Constitution were used in writing the United States Constitution.

The Massachusetts Constitution also had something the others did not have. It said that each town must provide free public education to all children. It also said that all children must attend school.

Work with three or four other students. Discuss the questions that follow. Then compare the answers of your group with those of your classmates.

1. Why do you think Massachusetts required each town to pay for the education of its children?
2. Should all children be required to attend school?
3. Should people who do not have children be required to pay taxes to support schools?
4. Most states now have laws about school attendance. What do the laws of your state require?
5. Do you think other laws about schools are needed? Why are they needed?

Why does education remain such an important issue for government?

Reviewing and Using the Lesson

1. What were some important ideas in the new state constitutions?
2. How did the state constitutions organize their governments?
3. How did the state constitutions limit the powers of their governments?
4. Why do you suppose most state constitutions began with a bill of rights?

Activities

1. Suppose that we did not have a national government. Each state would be a separate country. Each state might have its own army, its own money, and its own trade rules. Make a list of problems that might occur in this situation.
2. Find a copy of your state constitution. What is in the first part of the constitution? Does it have a bill of rights? Does the constitution say anything about education? Report your findings to your class.
3. Find one or more Native American tribal constitutions. How are they similar or different from the United States Constitution?

UNIT 2

How did the Framers write our Constitution?

UNIT

2

How did the Framers write our Constitution?

Since they had declared their independence, the Founders needed to create a new government for all the states of the new nation. They did this by creating our first constitution, known as the Articles of Confederation. The problems of the national government under the Articles of Confederation led the Founders to decide to write a new constitution.

The United States Constitution was written by the delegates who attended the Philadelphia Convention. These delegates are known as the Framers of the Constitution. The convention lasted from May to September 1787. The fifty-five Framers worked together for four months. The new Constitution they wrote has lasted more than two hundred years!

Some of the Framers were from states with large populations and some from states with small populations. Some were from the North, which had few slaves, and some from the South, where there were many slaves. These differences led to disagreements about what should be in the new Constitution.

This unit will help you understand why the Framers wrote the United States Constitution the way they did. You will read about the agreements and disagreements among the Framers. You will learn how the Framers made compromises to solve their disagreements.

KEY TOPICS

- Articles of Confederation
- Framers
- Great Compromise
- Philadelphia Convention
- three-fifths clause

LESSON
7

What was the first national government like?

LESSON PURPOSE

After the Declaration of Independence was signed, the Founders needed to create a new government for all the states of the new nation. They did this by creating our first constitution. It was called the Articles of Confederation.

LESSON OBJECTIVES

When you have finished this lesson, you should be able to

- ❑ describe the national government under the Articles of Confederation, and
- ❑ explain how the problems of the new government led the Founders to decide to write a new constitution.

TERMS TO KNOW

- Articles of Confederation
- confederation
- delegate
- Northwest Ordinance
- ordinance
- Shays' Rebellion

If you had been a member of the Second Continental Congress, which would have been more important to you: setting up a national government or fighting the war against Great Britain? Why?

What kind of national government did the Founders create under the Articles of Confederation?

The Second Continental Congress met in Philadelphia in 1775 soon after the Revolutionary War with Great Britain started. It acted as the first government of the United States. It created an army and asked George Washington to lead it. It managed the war against Great Britain. It also approved the Declaration of Independence on July 4, 1776. The Declaration told why the British colonies were separating from Great Britain and creating their own country.

The Second Continental Congress also asked each of the thirteen new states to develop a plan for its own government. These plans were called constitutions.

How did the Articles of Confederation organize the first national government?

Then, the Congress developed a plan for a national government over all the states. It was called the **Articles of Confederation**. It was sent to the states for their approval. It was our nation's first constitution. The Articles set up a loose union of states with equal powers. We call such a union a **confederation**.

The Founders faced two main problems when they wrote the Articles of Confederation.

1. The people feared a strong national government. They just had a revolution to get rid of a strong British government. They did not want another one like it. They felt that a strong national government might take away the rights of the states and the people.

2. The people were afraid that some states would have more power than other states in the new government.

What were the main problems faced by the Founders when they wrote the Articles of Confederation?

What was the problem with the way Congress raised money for the national government under the Articles of Confederation?

These fears influenced the Founders who wrote the Articles of Confederation. Therefore, they chose to set up a weak national government. It was a government with very limited powers.

Under the Articles, there were neither national courts nor a president. The power of government was in the Congress. The Articles did not give Congress very much power, either. For example, Congress could not raise money to run the government by directly taxing the people. Congress had to ask the states for money. The states gave money if and when they wanted to. The states had their own governments and made sure they kept most of the power for themselves.

Each state had one vote in Congress. The size of a state's population did not matter. States with more people had the same number of votes as states with far fewer people. Congress could not do anything important without having the approval of all the state governments.

After much debate, the states approved the Articles of Confederation. The Articles were in effect for seven years. Let's look at what the people were able to do under the Articles.

What was accomplished under the Articles of Confederation?

Even with their weaknesses, the Articles of Confederation were useful to the new nation. The national government was able to accomplish the following tasks:

- keeping the states together during the war against Great Britain,
- winning the war for independence,
- making a peace treaty with Great Britain, and
- preventing each state from conducting its own foreign affairs, making treaties, and declaring war.

The government under the Articles of Confederation passed the **Northwest Ordinance** of 1787. An **ordinance** is an order or law made by a government. This government order was a plan for adding new states. It allowed people living in the Northwest Territories—the land between the Mississippi River, the Great Lakes, and the Ohio River—to organize their own governments. When a territory had a large enough population, it could join the Union. The new states would be equals of the original states, not colonies. The Ordinance said that part of all public lands in these states must be set aside for public schools. It declared slavery unlawful in any new state in the Northwest Territories. The Ordinance also guaranteed freedom of religion, speech, and press.

What was the function of Congress under the Articles of Confederation?

Why did Daniel Shays and his followers rebel? What did they hope to gain?

What problems did the national government have under the Articles of Confederation?

When the Revolution was over, each state acted as a separate country. Each had its own interests. People did not think of themselves as citizens of the United States. They thought of themselves as citizens of their own states, such as Virginians, New Yorkers, or Georgians. Often the state governments did not cooperate with each other to solve common problems.

The national government under the Articles was weak. It did not have the power to unite the states. It did not have money, and it did not have the authority to get it. There were no courts to settle disputes among the states.

By 1786, there was little trade between the states or with other nations. It was hard for Americans to make a living. Many businesses were failing. Many people were in debt. Soldiers who had fought in the Revolutionary War still had not been paid.

Why was Shays' Rebellion an important event?

The states had their own problems. In Massachusetts, many farmers did not have any money. They could not trade their products in other states or countries.

When they could not pay their bills, they lost their farms and homes. Some were put in prison because they could not pay their bills. Many people protested because they felt this situation was unfair.

In 1786, more than one thousand angry farmers gathered under a leader named Daniel Shays. They were ready to fight the Massachusetts government. They shut down the courts to prevent the government from taking their property and jailing them. They tried to capture weapons to use in their struggle.

State troops stopped **Shays' Rebellion.** Many people were frightened by the rebellion. They worried that it might spread to other states.

How might the national government under the Articles of Confederation be improved?

The Founders knew that the Articles of Confederation had many weaknesses. The national government under the Articles was not effective. It was time to make improvements. Congress agreed and called for a meeting to be held in Philadelphia in 1787.

Each state was asked to send delegates. A **delegate** is someone whom you trust to represent your interests. The delegates were supposed to suggest ways to improve the Articles. Once they all got together, something else happened. They decided to put the Articles aside and start over again. The delegates then began to write a new constitution.

What did the delegates to the Philadelphia Convention decide to do about improving the Articles of Confederation?

Reviewing and Using the Lesson

1. Why did the Founders create a weak national government?
2. What did the first national government accomplish under the Articles of Confederation?
3. What were some problems under the Articles of Confederation?
4. Describe Shays' Rebellion. Why was it important?
5. What did the Northwest Ordinance of 1787 require of new states?
6. Why did the Founders decide to have a meeting in Philadelphia?

Activities

1. Learn more about the Northwest Ordinance. How did it help to provide education for all people? What rights did it protect? How did it prevent slavery? What effects did it have on the Native American tribes?
2. Learn more about Shays' Rebellion. Write a letter to a newspaper from the point of view of a farmer. Write a letter from the point of view of a property owner who was against the uprising.
3. Create a short play that shows one of the problems under the Articles of Confederation. Perform your play for the class.
4. Find out about other nations that are establishing new governments. Do their constitutions have any of the same problems as the Articles of Confederation? Use the internet or go to your library for your research. Share what you learn with the class.

LESSON

8

How was the Philadelphia Convention organized?

LESSON PURPOSE

In this lesson, you will learn about some important Framers who attended the Philadelphia Convention. You will also learn about some decisions that were made at the beginning of the convention.

LESSON OBJECTIVES

When you have finished this lesson, you should be able to explain

- ❑ the purpose of the Philadelphia Convention, and
- ❑ what decisions the Framers made before writing the Constitution.

TERMS TO KNOW

- Framers
- Philadelphia Convention

What Do You Think?

Who should participate in government?

Suppose a group of students at your school were given the task of creating a constitution for your student government. Meet in groups of about five students. Discuss the following questions. Be prepared to report your answers to the class.

1. Who should attend the meeting? Should each class have the right to send delegates? Why or why not?
2. Should some classes be able to send more delegates than others? Why or why not?
3. How should class delegates be selected? Why?
4. What qualifications should delegates have? Why?
5. What responsibilities should delegates have? Why?
6. Which basic ideas about government that you have studied did you apply in answering these questions?

Who should have the right to participate in government?

Who were the delegates to the Philadelphia Convention?

Who were the Framers?

The delegates to the Philadelphia Convention are known as the **Framers** of the United States Constitution. They are called the Framers because they organized and wrote, or "framed," our Constitution. Many of the Framers had been leaders during the American Revolution. About three-fourths had served in Congress. Most were leaders in their states.

The delegates were not chosen from all parts of the American population. Some were rich, but most were not. There were no poor people, no indentured servants, and no young people. All the Framers were men. Their average age was forty-two. There were no women among the delegates. There were no free black men or slaves. There were no Native Americans. Poor farmers—such as those who took part in Shays' Rebellion—were not present, nor were the citizens of Rhode Island. People in Rhode Island were so much against changing the Articles of Confederation that they refused to send any delegates!

What type of government did George Washington think the country needed?

Why is James Madison called the "Father of the Constitution"?

What role did Benjamin Franklin play at the Philadelphia Convention?

What did Thomas Paine contribute to the struggle for independence?

Why did Thomas Jefferson not attend the Philadelphia Convention?

Why did Patrick Henry not support the new Constitution?

Three important delegates to the convention were George Washington, James Madison, and Benjamin Franklin. George Washington was from Virginia. He was probably the most respected man in the country. As commander in chief of the American army during the Revolution, he was a great hero to most people. By 1787, he had retired to his plantation and would have liked to remain there. His friends urged him to attend the convention. They said his support was necessary to get a new constitution accepted by the people. Because Washington thought a stronger national government was necessary, he went to Philadelphia.

James Madison is often called the "Father of the Constitution." His ideas about government greatly influenced the other delegates. He had already developed a written plan for the new government that he brought to Philadelphia. It was known as the Virginia Plan, and it called for a strong national government. He helped put together compromises that solved some of the disagreements among the Framers. Madison took notes during the meetings. Much of what we know about the Philadelphia Convention is based on his notes.

Benjamin Franklin attended the convention as a delegate from Pennsylvania. He was eighty-one years old and in poor health. Like Washington, he was highly respected by Americans. Franklin had been a printer, inventor, and writer. He had also helped our country develop good relations with other nations. At the convention, he encouraged the delegates to cooperate with each other and work hard to settle their differences. His support of the Constitution was important to the other delegates.

If you had been a delegate to the Philadelphia Convention, what role might you have played? Why?

Who were some important Founders who were not at the convention?

At the time of the **Philadelphia Convention**, Thomas Jefferson and Thomas Paine were in France. Jefferson had written the Declaration of Independence. Paine had written *Common Sense*, an important book that helped get support for the Revolution. John Adams, a leader during the Revolution, was in Great Britain.

Other well-known Americans refused to go to the convention. Patrick Henry of Virginia was one of them. He feared that the delegates would try to create a strong national government. After the convention, Henry worked hard to convince the people to reject the Constitution.

What decisions did the delegates make at the start of the convention?

At the start of the convention, the Framers agreed on four things.

1. George Washington would serve as president of the convention.
2. Each state, large or small, would have one vote at the convention.
3. They would not do what Congress had asked them to do. They would not try to improve the Articles of Confederation. The Articles had too many weaknesses. They decided to write an entirely new constitution.
4. They would keep their discussions private. They decided that whatever was said at the meeting would remain a secret for thirty years.

There were good reasons for secrecy. The Framers believed they needed to speak freely. If people told others what they said, they would not feel as free to discuss their ideas. They would be less likely to change their minds during debate.

The Framers wanted the people to accept the new constitution. They feared that the people might not if they knew all the disagreements the Framers had during the writing.

Once the Framers reached these agreements, it was time to get down to work. It was time to create a constitution. In the next lessons, you will learn about some of the disagreements the Framers had and how they solved them.

Why did the delegates to the Philadelphia Convention decide to keep their discussions private?

Reviewing and Using the Lesson

1. Why did Congress call for the Philadelphia Convention?
2. Describe the members of the Philadelphia Convention as a group.
3. Who were some of the important Framers? Why are they called Framers?
4. At the start of the meeting, what important decisions did the Framers make? Why?

Activities

1. Imagine that you are a newspaper editor in 1787. Write an article in which you support or oppose keeping the debates secret.
2. Learn more about the Framers who are discussed in this lesson or other Framers. Role-play a television show and interview the Framers.
3. Draw a picture showing the Framers at work during the convention.

LESSON 9

How many representatives should each state have in Congress?

LESSON PURPOSE

The delegates to the Philadelphia Convention agreed to write a new constitution. They wanted the new constitution to provide a stronger national government. One difficult thing they had to decide was how many representatives each state would be allowed to send to Congress. In this lesson, you will discuss this question. You will learn how the Framers solved the problem.

LESSON OBJECTIVES

When you have finished this lesson, you should be able to explain why the Framers organized our Congress the way they did.

TERMS TO KNOW

- Great Compromise
- House of Representatives
- Senate

Why were states with small populations afraid of states with large populations?

What was the conflict between the large states and the small states?

How many representatives should each state be able to send to Congress? This was one of the hardest questions the Framers had to answer.

Delegates from states with small populations were afraid. They did not want the larger states to have more votes in Congress than they had. If that happened, the large states would have more power. They would control the new national government.

Delegates from small states argued that each state should have the same number of representatives in Congress. Delegates from states with large populations said that was not fair. A state with more people should have more votes in Congress.

During the long debates, the Framers could not reach a decision on this issue. Neither side was willing to give in. The delegates were almost ready to quit and go home. Finally, they formed a special committee to try to find a solution. One delegate from each state was on the committee.

Critical Thinking Exercise

How many representatives in Congress should each state have?

Work in small groups of delegates. Each group should study the bar graph on the next page. You may draw a chart like the one on page 74, or your teacher might give you a handout. Read the questions, and write your answers on your chart.

STEP 1 There are seven small states and six large states. Which states are they? Write their names in column one on your chart.

STEP 2 Look at the graph and figure out the population of each state. Write these numbers in column two on your chart.

STEP 3 Suppose each state sends only one representative to Congress, and write the number one in column three on your chart.

STEP 4 Now, suppose it is decided that each state would have one representative for every 30,000 people in the state. How many representatives would each state have? Divide the population by 30,000. Write these numbers in column four on your chart.

STEP 5 Add the numbers in each column. Put your answers in the total boxes.

Discuss and answer the following questions

1. If it were decided that there should be one representative for each state, how many representatives would all the small states have together? How many would all the large states have together?
2. If it were decided that representation should be based on the population of each state, how many representatives would the small states have together? How many would the large states have together?
3. In each state, how many people would each representative represent?
4. Why would the small states favor the idea of having one representative for the whole state?
5. Why would the large states favor the idea of having one representative for every 30,000 people in the state?

Make a decision based on your discussion

1. Should the number of representatives that each state sends to Congress be based on its population? Or, should each state send one representative?

2. What would happen if you divide Congress into two parts or houses, so that in one house, each state would have one representative, and in the other house, each state would have representatives based on its population?

3. What might be the advantages of dividing Congress into two houses as described in question two? What might be the disadvantages?

Explain your group's point of view to the class. Give reasons for your group's decisions. The whole class should take part in the discussion and reach an agreement on the best way to solve the problem of representation in Congress.

Estimated populations of the thirteen states (1787)

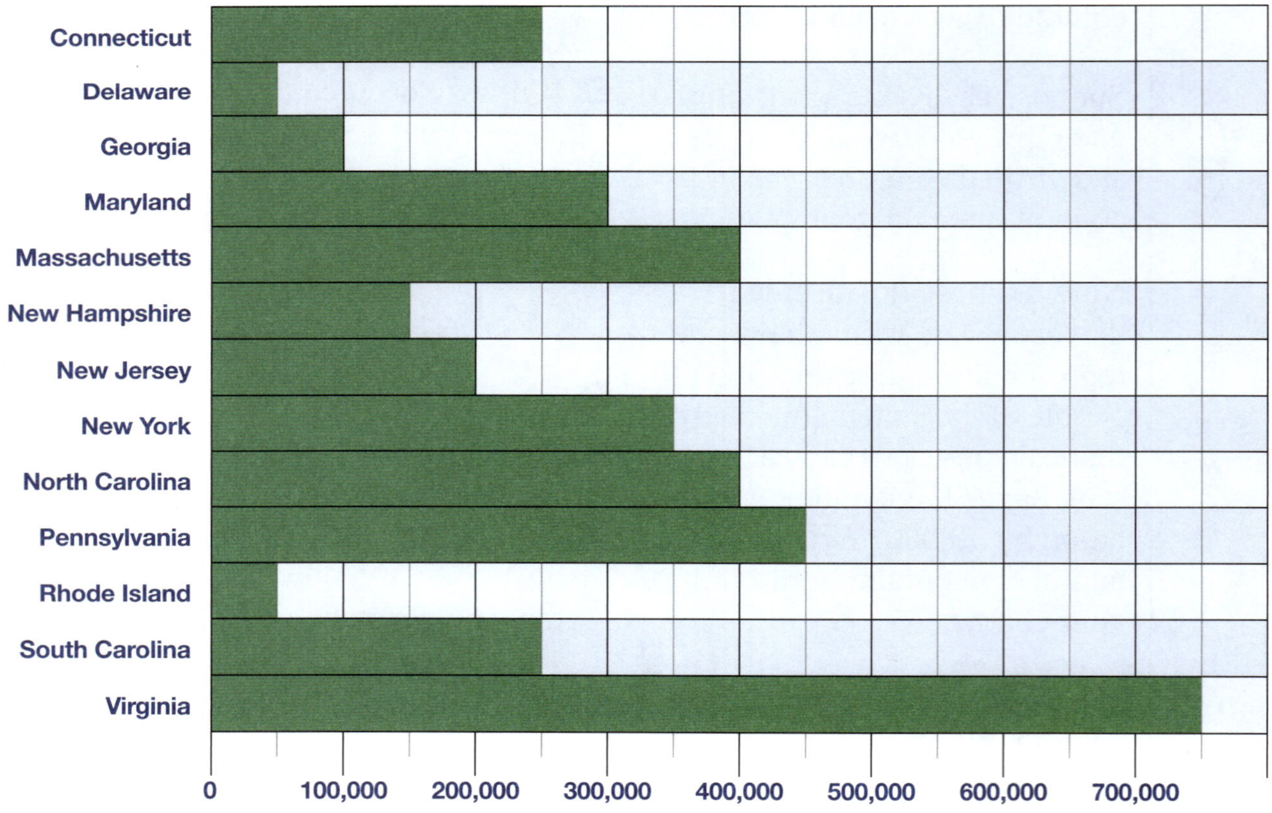

How many representatives should a state have?

▼ STEP 1 List the SMALL STATES	▼ STEP 2 List the population	▼ STEP 3 List one representative for each state	▼ STEP 4 List the number of representatives by population (30,000 people = 1 representative)
1			
2			
3			
4			
5			
6			
7			
STEP 5 ▶ Totals			

List the LARGE STATES	List the population	List one representative for each state	List the number of representatives by population (30,000 people = 1 representative)
1			
2			
3			
4			
5			
6			
Totals			

How does this picture show representation in the Senate? How would this plan help the smaller states?

What was the Great Compromise?

Compromise is a way of dealing with a problem. Each side must be willing to give up something in order to solve the problem. Both sides have to agree on the solution. The Framers knew that they had to find a way to solve the problem of representation. They wanted a compromise the delegates would accept.

They appointed a committee to make a plan. The result of the committee's work is known as the **Great Compromise**. It is the plan the delegates accepted for representation in Congress. These are the main parts of the Great Compromise.

- Congress would have two parts, or houses: the **Senate** and the **House of Representatives**.
- Each state, large or small, would have two representatives in the Senate.
- In the House of Representatives, the number of representatives from each state would be based on the number of people living in that state.

This agreement meant that each state would have equal power in the Senate. The states with more people would have more power in the House of Representatives. A law could not be passed unless a majority in both houses voted for it. This meant that large and small states could check each other's power. The Great Compromise protected the interests of both small and large states.

Some Framers did not like the compromise. It was hard for them to give up what they wanted. Nevertheless, the delegates voted and the Great Compromise was agreed upon.

How does this picture show representation in the House of Representatives? How would this plan help the larger states?

Reviewing and Using the Lesson

1. Why was it hard for the Framers to agree on how many representatives a state should be able to send to Congress?

2. How did the Great Compromise solve the problem of representation in Congress?

Activities

1. Find the names of the people who represent your state in the United States Senate.

2. How many representatives does your state have in the United States House of Representatives? What is the number of your congressional district? Who is your representative? Does everyone in your class have the same representative? Why or why not?

3. Find a map of the United States that shows the number of representatives the states have in the House of Representatives. Which states have the most members in the House of Representatives? Which have the fewest? How many people does one representative represent? See if you can find your congressional district on the map.

4. Think of a problem in your school that causes disagreements among your classmates. Make a list of things to consider when you compromise or negotiate. What things should you do? What things should you not do? Then, try working out a compromise with your classmates.

LESSON 10

What did the Framers do about the problem of slavery?

LESSON PURPOSE

The Framers at the Philadelphia Convention faced another important issue. That issue was the question of slavery. Many colonists had depended on the labor of enslaved people for more than one hundred fifty years. The delegates from the Northern and Southern states could not agree about what to do. In this lesson, you will learn about the compromise the Framers reached on this issue.

LESSON OBJECTIVES

When you have finished this lesson, you should be able to explain why the Framers agreed to the three-fifths clause.

TERMS TO KNOW

- abolish
- Civil War
- slave trade
- three-fifths clause

What was the slave trade?

When our nation was founded, the slave trade had been practiced in many parts of the world for thousands of years. People in America had kept men, women, and children as indentured servants from the time of the first British colonies. But, the first people brought to the colonies specifically to be slaves were Africans.

Some of these African people were captured in tribal wars and sold to slave traders. Others were captured by the slave traders themselves. The slave traders brought the Africans to the colonies in large sailing ships. Life aboard the ships was terrible. Many people died. Once in the colonies, the slave traders sold the people they had captured and transported.

In America, slaves were treated as if they were property, something that you can own, buy, and sell. Families were often broken up, and children were sold separately from their parents.

When the Founders signed the Declaration of Independence, there were about half a million people kept as slaves in the colonies. Before the Revolutionary War, there were slaves in every colony, in both the North and South.

Most people in the Southern states were farmers. Ninety percent of the slaves were in the Southern states. Plantation owners used the people that they kept as slaves to work their land. Crops such as cotton, rice, and indigo required a lot of labor. Plantation owners became dependent on slave labor for their profits.

People in the Northern states made their living in a number of different ways. They worked as farmers, fishers, merchants, and bankers. Others owned shops or worked in them. Most people in the North did not own slaves. Some Northerners, however, made their living in the **slave trade**, buying people in Africa and selling them mostly to Southerners.

What did the Framers think about slavery?

The Framers came to Philadelphia with different opinions about slavery. Many of the delegates, including some from the South, believed that keeping people as slaves was wrong.

Most Southern delegates, however, wanted to protect the slaveholders. The large plantation owners depended upon slave labor for their living. These delegates said they would not support the Constitution if it abolished slavery. To **abolish** means to put an end to something. They said their states would refuse to be part of the new national government. The Framers had three main questions to resolve.

1. Should they allow the slave trade to continue?

2. Should they count slaves as part of a state's population? If they did, it would increase the number of representatives from Southern states in Congress. This would give the Southern states more power.

Why was there a conflict between Northern and Southern Framers about slavery?

3. What should happen to slaves who ran away to states that did not allow slavery?

Let's look at how the Framers dealt with these questions.

What compromises did the Framers make?

After long, hard debates and discussions, the Framers agreed on several compromises about slavery.

The compromises were accepted by both the Northern and Southern states. The main purpose of these compromises was to get the Southern states to agree to be part of the new government. As with all compromises, neither side got everything it wanted.

The Northern states agreed that the Constitution would allow slavery to continue. The national government was not allowed to end the slave trade until 1808. Slaves who escaped to other states had to be returned.

Slave populations of the thirteen original states (from the 1790 census)

Total state population in **black**
State population of slaves in *red*

State	Total population	Slave population
Connecticut	237,655	2,764
Delaware	59,096	8,887
Georgia	82,548	29,264
Maryland	319,728	103,036
Massachusetts	378,556	0
New Hampshire	141,899	158
New Jersey	184,139	11,423
New York	340,241	21,324
North Carolina	395,005	100,572
Pennsylvania	433,611	3,737
Rhode Island	69,112	948
South Carolina	249,073	107,094
Virginia	747,550	292,627

The Southern states agreed that Congress would have the power to control trade between the states. This would help Northern businesses.

Finally, Northern and Southern delegates agreed upon another compromise. The **three-fifths clause** gave Southern states the right to count three-fifths of their slaves for the purpose of representation in Congress. In this compromise, the Southern states could send more representatives to Congress than if they were not allowed to count any slaves at all. They also had to pay more direct taxes than if they had not counted the slaves as part of the population.

Because of this compromise, the Southern states agreed to support the Constitution. They would be part of the new nation. The Constitution nowhere uses the word *slave*. Some people say this is because the Framers were ashamed of slavery.

How did slavery end in the United States?

Slavery continued in the United States for almost another eighty years. It ended only as a result of the Civil War. The **Civil War** was the war between the Northern and Southern states.

Soon after the Civil War, the Constitution was changed. The Thirteenth Amendment freed people from slavery. Other amendments gave former slaves the rights of citizens. However, these amendments did not end the unfair treatment of the newly freed slaves.

How did the three-fifths clause work for representation and direct taxes?

Reviewing and Using the Lesson

1. Why did the Northern and Southern states have different ideas about slavery?
2. What compromise did the Framers reach about slavery?
3. Why did the Framers compromise on this important issue?

Activities

1. Imagine you are a delegate to the Philadelphia Convention. Write a letter home to your family in which you explain your position on the slavery question.
2. Learn what life was like on board a slave ship. Share what you learned with the class.
3. Imagine you help a runaway slave escape to freedom. Write a story about what you would do. In your story, describe what the Constitution says about returning runaway slaves.

UNIT 3

How does the Constitution organize our government?

UNIT

3

How does the Constitution organize our government?

In most other nations in 1787, the government was the master of the people. The government held all the power. Even today, many governments are still the masters of their people. People living under these governments have very few of the rights we have.

The Framers knew when they created our government that they faced a difficult problem. They wanted to create a stronger national government. But, they also worried about creating a government with too much power. A government with too much power might become our master instead of our servant.

Try to imagine how you would solve this problem if you were one of the Framers. Suppose you were creating a new government for our country. You know you have to give the government power over your life, liberty, and property. You are afraid of giving the government so much power.

How can you plan your government so it will remain the servant of the people? How can you organize it so that its powers will be limited and it will not become your master? In this unit, you will learn how the Framers solved this problem.

KEY TOPICS

- checks and balances
- Electoral College
- executive branch
- federal system
- judicial branch
- judicial review
- legislative branch
- preamble
- separation of powers
- supremacy clause
- "We the People"

LESSON 11

What basic ideas about government are included in the Preamble to the Constitution?

LESSON PURPOSE

The Framers wrote an introduction, also called a *preamble*, to the Constitution. The Preamble states the purposes of our Constitution. It includes some basic ideas about government that you have studied in this book.

LESSON OBJECTIVES

When you finish this lesson, you should be able to explain the purposes of our government contained in the Preamble to the Constitution.

TERMS TO KNOW

- blessings of liberty
- common defense
- domestic tranquility
- establish
- general welfare
- justice
- ordain
- Preamble

What Do You Think?

What should be the purposes of government?

Before you learn about the purposes stated in the Preamble, let's examine your own ideas. Then you can compare your ideas with those in the Constitution. You might find that you and the Framers have many of the same ideas.

Work with a partner or in a group of three to five students. Discuss the questions that follow. Be prepared to share your ideas with the class.

1. What is a purpose?
2. Why is it important to know what your own purposes are?
3. Why is it important to know what the purposes of a government are?
4. List five or six purposes that you think a government should have.
5. Explain why you think each of the purposes you have listed for government is important.

A nuclear power plant and wind turbines. Do you think government should regulate these sources of energy? Why or why not?

How can citizens show that they give approval to be governed by the Constitution?

Why does the Preamble say "We the People ... do ordain and establish this Constitution for the United States of America"?

In 1787, the Framers wrote and signed the Constitution. The Preamble to the Constitution says that "We the People of the United States ... do **ordain** [give official approval] and **establish** [accept] this Constitution for the United States of America." This means that the Constitution was approved by the people of the United States and that they agreed to live under the government it created. Each generation of Americans—including yours—must give its approval or consent to live under the government created by the Constitution.

- How do you and other Americans show that you consent to be governed under the Constitution?
- How do you, as one of the people, ordain and establish the Constitution?

There are many ways of answering these questions. One way is by willingly obeying the laws. Another way to show your consent is by repeating the Pledge of Allegiance. When you are older, you can give your consent by voting, serving on a jury, or holding public office. You also give consent when you take part in solving your community's problems. Taking your place as a citizen, one of "We the People," means that you consent to live under the Constitution.

Critical Thinking Exercise

What ideas are expressed in the Preamble?

Preamble to the Constitution of the United States

We the People of the United States, in order to form a more perfect union, establish **justice**, *insure* **domestic tranquility**, *provide for the* **common defense**, *promote the* **general welfare**, *and secure the* **blessings of liberty** *to ourselves and our posterity, do ordain and establish this Constitution for the United States of America.*

The **Preamble** to the Constitution explains who created the Constitution and the basic purposes of our government. "We the People" are the first words in the Preamble. These words are very important. They show that the power to govern belongs to the people. The people established the Constitution. They used it to create a government to protect their rights and their welfare.

The ideas in the Preamble are so important that you should study them carefully. To do this, first read the entire Preamble.

The Preamble is made up of many words that might be hard to understand when you first read them. But if you study them, you will find they are not that difficult.

Let's examine the basic ideas in the Preamble to see how important they are to all of us. To do this, your class may work in small groups. Each group should study one part of the Preamble.

Why are the first words of the Constitution, "We the People," so important?

Which words in the Preamble give government the right to organize military forces?

We the People...

GROUP 1 do ordain and establish this Constitution for the United States of America

GROUP 2 establish justice

GROUP 3 insure domestic tranquility

GROUP 4 provide for the common defense

GROUP 5 promote the general welfare

GROUP 6 secure the blessings of liberty

Each group should answer the following questions about the part it is studying. Be prepared to explain your group's answers to the rest of the class.

1. What do the words that your group studied mean? Give an example.
2. Why is the part of the Preamble that your group studied important?
3. What does the part your group studied have to do with protecting your rights and the common good?

Reviewing and Using the Lesson

1. Some people have said the most important words in our Constitution are the first three words of the Preamble. These are the words "We the People." Explain why you agree or disagree with this opinion.

2. In your own words, explain what *establishing justice* means. Why is this an important purpose of government?

3. Explain the difference between *ensuring domestic tranquility* and *providing for the common defense*.

4. What is the *general welfare*? What are some ways to promote the general welfare?

5. What are some of the *blessings of liberty* that you enjoy? How can you help to make sure that future generations will also enjoy them?

6. How can you and other Americans show that you consent to live under the Constitution?

Activities

1. The people who worked on writing the Preamble were William Samuel Johnson, Alexander Hamilton, James Madison, Rufus King, and Gouverneur Morris. Learn more about these men. Share what you learned with the class.

2. Work with a partner to create a skit. One of you should portray Patrick Henry, who said the Framers did not have the right to speak the language of "We the People" instead of "We the States." The other student should portray Gouverneur Morris defending the position of the Framers in the use of the words "We the People." Perform your skit for the class.

3. Create six symbols to represent each of the six parts of the Preamble. In your own words, write a sentence that tells what each symbol means. Use the six symbols to create a bulletin board for your classroom.

LESSON 12

How does the Constitution limit the powers of our government?

LESSON PURPOSE

The Framers wanted to limit the powers of our national government. They wanted to be sure that no one group of people in government would have too much power. So, they divided the powers of government among three groups or branches. In this lesson, you will learn more about the separation of powers and checks and balances.

LESSON OBJECTIVES

When you have finished this lesson, you should be able to explain

- ❑ why the Framers separated the powers of our government and
- ❑ how the Constitution balances and checks the powers of each branch of government.

TERMS TO KNOW

- balancing powers
- branches
- checking powers
- executive power
- judicial power
- legislative power
- separation of powers
- United States Supreme Court

Critical Thinking Exercise

How would you organize your government?

Suppose you want to create a government for your class. Think about how you might organize that government. It would need to have the following powers:

1. Power to make rules. This is called **legislative power**.
2. Power to carry out and enforce the rules. This is called **executive power**.
3. Power to settle disagreements about the rules. This includes the power to say what the rules mean. This is called **judicial power**.

Think about how you might distribute these powers in your class government. Work in small groups and answer the questions below. Be prepared to share your answers with the class.

1. Suppose you decide to give all the powers of your class government to one group of students. What would be the advantages and disadvantages of doing this?
2. Suppose you decide to give the power to three different groups of students. You divide the powers of your government among them. What would be the advantages and disadvantages of doing this?

How might you use the idea of separation of powers to organize a school government?

What ideas did the Framers use to limit the power of government?

When the Framers organized our national government, they knew they needed to limit its powers. The Framers did this by dividing the government into three parts. They called these parts the three **branches** of government. They gave certain powers to each branch.

- **Legislative branch** The Framers gave this branch the power to make laws. They called our national legislature "Congress." Congress has two parts or houses. They are the Senate and the House of Representatives.
- **Executive branch** The Framers gave this branch the power to carry out and enforce the laws made by Congress. The president is the head of this branch.
- **Judicial branch** The Framers gave this branch the power to settle disagreements about what the laws mean. The **United States Supreme Court** is the highest court in this branch.

What else did the Framers do to limit the power of government?

The Framers knew that governments often gain too much power. When they do, they can violate the rights of the people. They work for the selfish interests of a few people instead of for the common good. They do not treat people fairly.

The Framers wanted to make sure this could not happen. They separated and balanced the powers among the different branches. Then they gave each branch a way to check the use of power by the other branches. The Framers believed that the way they organized the government was the best way to protect the rights and welfare of the people.

The Framers knew from history that constitutional governments are often divided into different branches. **Separation of powers** means to divide the power of government among its branches. The Framers used the idea of separation of powers as one way to limit the power of government.

The Framers also knew that it was not enough just to separate the powers of government. If you gave too much power to one branch, it might control the others. The Framers believed that the powers of government needed to be balanced among the different branches. **Balancing powers** means that no one government branch is given so much power that it can completely control the other branches.

The Framers used one more way to limit the power of government. They gave each branch ways to check the other branches. **Checking powers** means that each branch can stop the other branches from making final decisions or from taking certain actions. For example, Congress has the power to make laws. The president can stop

How is power balanced among the different branches of government?

or control this power by refusing to approve a bill passed by Congress. But, the bill might still become law. Two-thirds of the members of Congress would have to vote to make it a law. Suppose the bill does become law. The judicial branch has the power to check Congress and the president. If a case is brought before them, the courts have the power to say that a certain law is not allowed by the Constitution.

Finally, the Tenth Amendment to the Constitution says that the powers that are not given to the national government are to be kept by the state governments or the people. States can use these powers as they wish. However, they cannot do things that violate laws made by Congress or the Constitution. The following are some things state governments have the powers to do.

- They can create and run public school systems.
- They can make laws protecting people's lives, liberty, and property.
- They can create law enforcement agencies and courts to try people accused of breaking state laws.
- They can organize and run elections for people running for positions in their governments and the national government.
- They can give areas within them, such as towns, cities, and counties, the right to organize and run their own governments.

How does the judicial branch check the power of the executive and legislative branches?

Reviewing and Using the Lesson

1. What are the three branches of our government? What power does each branch have?
2. Why did the Framers separate the powers of our government? How are they separated?
3. Why did the Framers balance the powers of our government?
4. Why did the Framers provide ways for each branch of our government to check the powers of the other branches? Give an example of how one branch can check the power of another.

Activities

1. Write a short letter to a friend. Describe what you have learned about the separation of powers and checks and balances. Tell why you think these ideas are important. Share your letter with the class.
2. Draw a diagram. In your diagram, show your understanding of how separation of powers and checks and balances work. Share your diagram with the class.
3. Find newspaper or magazine articles that report examples of the use of checks and balances. Share your articles with the class.
4. Watch the news on television. Report to the class any story about one branch of government checking another branch.

LESSON

13

What is the legislative branch?

LESSON PURPOSE

You have learned that the legislative branch makes our laws. Our national legislature is Congress. In this lesson, you will learn about the powers of Congress. You will learn something about how Congress makes laws. You will also learn how our Constitution limits the powers of Congress.

LESSON OBJECTIVES

When you have finished this lesson, you should be able to

- ❑ explain how Congress is organized,
- ❑ describe the powers it has,
- ❑ say how its powers are limited, and
- ❑ explain how a law is made.

TERMS TO KNOW

- Article I
- bill
- Congress
- unconstitutional
- veto

What is Congress?

Congress is the legislative branch of our national government. It makes our nation's laws. As you have learned, the Framers created two houses of Congress. The two houses are the Senate and the House of Representatives.

Senate

Senators must be at least thirty years old. They must have been citizens of the United States for at least nine years, and they must live in the state that they represent. Senators are elected to serve for six years.

Each state sends two people to the Senate. Today, the United States Senate has one hundred senators.

House of Representatives

Representatives must be at least twenty-five years old. They must have been citizens for at least seven years, and they must live in the state they represent. Representatives are elected to serve for two years.

The number of representatives each state can send to the House is based on its population. Currently, each member of the House represents about 710,000 people. When the Constitution was written, each member represented 30,000 people. The total number of representatives is now limited to 435. There are six representatives from other parts of our country: the District of Columbia, American Samoa, the Commonwealth of Puerto Rico, Guam, the Commonwealth of the Northern Mariana Islands, and the United States Virgin Islands. In 2019, California had the most people. California sent fifty-three representatives to the House. Wyoming had the smallest population. Wyoming and six other states each sent one representative to the House.

What powers does Congress have?

Article I of the Constitution lists the powers of Congress. Some of these powers are very specific. For example, Congress has the power to

- tax the people,
- raise an army and navy to defend our nation,
- declare war,
- create a court system, and
- coin money.

Other powers of Congress are very general. The Constitution gives Congress the power to

- pass all laws that are necessary and proper to carry out its responsibilities. For example, Congress passed the Civil Rights Acts to prevent unfair discrimination against some citizens.

What does the legislative branch do?

- provide for the general welfare of the United States. For example, Congress created the National Institutes of Health to support medical research on health issues and to find cures for those who are sick.

How does Congress make a law?

Congress provides for the general welfare by passing laws that help people. Suppose that you, a member of Congress, the president, or some group with an interest, has an idea for a new law. How does the idea become a law? Here are the basic steps that must be followed.

1. **Write a bill** A member of Congress must agree that the idea is good. Then, he or she writes a proposal for the law, which is called a bill. A **bill** is a proposed law.

2. **Go to committee** Congress has committees that deal with different areas of the people's needs. A committee will examine the bill. The members of the committee discuss the bill, and then they might rewrite it, change some parts, or decide that it is not a good bill.

3. **Get a majority vote of Congress** When the bill is ready, the member of Congress who wrote the bill must

What steps does Congress need to follow to make a new law?

get a majority of members to vote for it. If the member is a senator, the bill goes to the Senate first. If she or he is a representative, it goes to the House of Representatives first. Then the bill goes to the other house for a vote.

4 **Get the president to approve the bill** If the bill passes in both houses, Congress must send the bill to the president. If the president approves the bill and signs it, it becomes a law. If the president refuses to sign the bill and sends it back to Congress, this is a **veto**. The bill can still become a law if two-thirds of all the members of each house of Congress votes to pass it over the president's veto.

How does the Constitution limit the powers of Congress?

The Constitution and Bill of Rights limit the powers of Congress. They list the kinds of laws that Congress may not make. For example, Congress may not make a law that unfairly and unnecessarily limits your freedom to speak.

Suppose Congress passed a bill saying you cannot criticize the national government. Then the president signed the bill and it became a law. How might this law be overturned? How are your rights protected?

The Supreme Court has the power to declare a law made by Congress unconstitutional. **Unconstitutional** means that

Why are the powers of Congress limited by the Constitution?

the Constitution does not give Congress the right to pass such a law. If the Supreme Court says this, then the law cannot be enforced. It is no longer a law. This is another check on Congress.

What are the responsibilities of senators and representatives?

Members of Congress are responsible for making laws that protect our rights and promote our welfare. To make laws, members of Congress first must learn about the problems of our country. There are groups with special interests that try to convince members of Congress to make laws that benefit their groups. Congress must find ways to deal with the problems that concern these groups, as well as the people as a whole. Senators and representatives talk to the people in their states and districts. They read letters sent by citizens. They listen to debates and attend committee meetings.

Making good laws is not easy. A bill might help some people while it harms others. Members of Congress must decide whether to vote for or against each bill. The next class participation activity will help you understand how difficult it can be to decide if a bill deserves support.

Critical Thinking Exercise

How should Representative Smith vote?

Suppose that Representative Smith is visiting your community to seek advice and opinions. She has arranged a public hearing on Thursday night at seven o'clock. She has invited the people who live in her district to attend the hearing. She is hoping for a good turnout. Representative Smith wants to find out if she should vote for a bill that would prevent smoking in public places.

Getting ready for the public hearing

Read the story and answer the questions that follow it. Prepare to play the role of one of the groups described after the story. Each group should prepare a presentation to make at the public hearing. Representative Smith and her staff will ask your opinion about a bill in Congress.

Representative Smith makes a decision

Smoking cigarettes is a national problem. Studies have shown that smoking is dangerous to everyone's health. Even breathing smoke from someone else's cigarette is dangerous. Each year, thousands of Americans die from smoking cigarettes.

Many farmers in Representative Smith's congressional district are involved in growing tobacco. Many other people make their living by working in factories that make tobacco products.

There is a bill in Congress that would forbid smoking in public places. Representative Smith knows smoking is dangerous and costly. She also knows that if she votes for the bill, the tobacco industry will suffer. Many people will lose their jobs, and some businesses will fail.

Representative Smith must decide how to vote on the bill. Should she vote against the bill to protect the jobs of the people in her district? Should she vote for the bill because she believes smoking is dangerous to people's health? The public hearing will help Representative Smith decide how to vote.

Representatives are supposed to support laws that protect people's rights. They are also supposed to support laws that serve the common good.

To make a good and fair decision, what issues does Representative Smith have to consider?

What rights are involved in this situation?

1. Which rights do you think are most important? Why?

2. What is the common good in this situation? Explain your answer.

Group 1: Representative Smith and Her Staff

Representative Smith must decide if she will vote "yes" or "no" on the bill. Before she decides, she and her staff want to know what the people in her district think about the problem. Representative Smith wants to speak with the groups that have valuable information about the situation. After she hears from the people she represents, she will make a decision.

Group 2: Tobacco Growers and Processors

You earn a living by growing and processing tobacco, just as your families have done for generations. If Representative Smith supports the bill, many people will lose their jobs. Some people will lose their businesses and their way of life.

Group 3: Citizens for Freedom

You believe that adults should be allowed to make their own lifestyle choices. You think that this bill would limit people's freedom to make their own decisions about their health and smoking.

How can Representative Smith make a good and fair decision when people in her district want her to support different things?

Group 4: Citizens for a Smoke-Free Environment

You think that smoking in public places is a serious problem. Smoking in public violates the rights of nonsmokers who are forced to breathe secondhand smoke.

Group 5: Citizens for Better Health

You think that putting limits on smoking in public would help improve everyone's health. All citizens carry the costs of healthcare.

Taking part in the public hearing

A member of each group may tell Representative Smith the group's opinion about the proposed law. That member may also give her advice on how to vote on the issue. Then, Representative Smith and her staff will discuss the problem, decide what to do, and explain their decision.

Talking it over

1. Do you agree with Representative Smith's decision? Why or why not?
2. Why might citizens disagree about which responsibility is more important for their representative to carry out?
3. In what other ways could Representative Smith carry out her responsibilities in this situation?
4. Did you change your own opinion after listening to all the groups? If you did, what argument convinced you?

Reviewing and Using the Lesson

1. What information will you find in Article I of the Constitution?
2. What does the legislative branch of our government do?
3. Name the two houses of Congress.
4. Make a list of some of the powers that the Constitution grants to Congress.
5. List and explain the steps by which a bill becomes a law.
6. What are some limits on the powers of Congress?

Activities

1. Find a recent newspaper article about Congress. Be prepared to talk about the issues in the article with your class.
2. The Constitution says that every ten years, the government must count the number of people in the country. This is called a census. Find out how the census is used to determine how many representatives a state may send to the House of Representatives.
3. Decorate your classroom by creating a picture gallery that shows the current senators from your state and the representative from your district. Write something about each person, and include this information in your gallery. Learn about some of the bills they have written or sponsored. Ask your teacher to invite your member of Congress to your classroom.
4. Write about the duties and privileges held by the six non-voting members of the House of Representatives. What are the similarities and differences between these members and the 435 voting members of the House? What, if anything, would you change about the non-voting members' duties and privileges?
5. Divide your class into two "houses." Ask each student or small group of students in each house to write a bill proposing a policy for your classroom. The writers of each bill should present it to their own house for a vote. If it passes, it should be presented to the other house for a vote. If the bills pass in both houses, send them to your teacher, who will act as president and approve or veto the bill.

What is the executive branch?

LESSON PURPOSE

You already learned that the executive branch carries out and enforces the laws passed by Congress. The president is the head of the executive branch. In this lesson, you will learn about the powers of the president. You will also learn how Congress can check the powers of the president.

LESSON OBJECTIVES

When you have finished this lesson, you should be able to

- ❑ describe how the executive branch is organized,
- ❑ identify the powers of this branch, and
- ❑ explain some of the limits on its powers.

TERMS TO KNOW

- appoint
- Article II
- budget
- commander in chief
- Electoral College
- impeach
- treaty

What is the system for selecting the president of the United States?

How did the Framers create the executive branch?

The executive branch of our government carries out and enforces the laws passed by Congress. For example, Congress might pass a law to build a highway across the country. The executive branch has to carry out the law.

The president of the United States is the head of the executive branch. The Framers had many discussions about how much power to give to the president. They did not want to make the executive branch too weak or too strong.

The Framers wanted to do two things. They wanted to give the president enough power to carry out and enforce the laws. But, they did not want to give the president too much power. If they did, a president might be able to gain unlimited power. With unlimited power, the president might become a dictator.

Article II of the Constitution establishes the executive branch. Article II lists the duties and powers of the president.

How is the president selected?

Every four years on the Tuesday following the first Monday in November, voters go to their polling places and cast their votes for the president and vice president of the United States. Their votes will be counted, but the results will not guarantee that the candidate with the most votes will become the president.

To select the president and vice president, the Framers of the Constitution proposed what is now called the **Electoral College**.

When people vote for the president, they are actually voting for electors who are pledged to vote for the candidate who wins most of the people's votes.

Each state has a number of electors equal to the number of U.S. senators, two for each state, plus the number of U.S. representatives, which varies according to the state's population. For example, Wyoming has two senators and one representative. So, it has three votes in the Electoral College. California has two senators and fifty-three representatives. So, it has fifty-five votes in the Electoral College.

The Electoral College includes 538 electors, 535 for the total number of members in Congress, and three electors who represent Washington, D.C. States with large populations have more electoral votes than states with small populations. A candidate must have 270 of the total 538 electoral votes to become president.

Because of the way the Electoral College is organized, there have been five times in our history when the candidate with the most votes for president did not win the election.

If no candidate gets a majority of votes in the Electoral College, the House of Representatives selects the president by majority vote. Each state, no matter how many people it has, is allowed one vote.

Although the Electoral College is complicated, the Framers thought it was the best solution for selecting the president during the time that they created the new government.

What Do You Think?

Should the candidate with the most votes win?

Many people in our country believe that the candidate with the most votes should automatically become president. Some people want to change the electoral system. Do you agree or disagree? Explain why or why not.

A meeting of Maryland's electoral college during the 2012 presidential election. Do you think we should change the electoral system? Why or why not?

What are the powers of presidents? How are these powers limited?

What are the powers and duties of the president?

The Framers gave the president many powers and duties. Some of these powers and duties are listed below.

The president has the power to

- act as the **commander in chief** of the armed forces. The military must obey the orders of the president.
- make treaties. A **treaty** is an official agreement between two or more countries. Treaties must have the advice and consent of the Senate.
- appoint ambassadors, with the consent of the Senate. The job of an ambassador is to represent the United States in another country. To **appoint** means to choose or name someone for an office or duty.
- appoint judges to the Supreme Court, with the consent of the Senate; appoint other officials of the United States.
- grant pardons for crimes against the United States.

The president must protect the Constitution. The president must also carry out the duties of the office. The president has the duty to

- act as the head of the executive branch. There are many departments, or offices, within the executive branch. The president must make sure that these departments carry out and enforce the laws.

- suggest laws and policies. The president may ask the Congress to pass certain laws. Every year the president prepares a budget. The **budget** is a plan for how to spend the nation's money. The president sends the budget to Congress for its approval.

- set policy for dealing with other countries in the world. The president is responsible for dealing with other countries.

How does the Constitution limit the powers of the president?

The Framers were careful to limit the powers of the president. They made the president share most powers with Congress. Here are some examples of how Congress can check the powers of the president.

- **Appointment** The president has the power to appoint people to important jobs in the executive and judicial branches. The Senate has to approve the person before he or she may have the job.

- **Treaties** The Senate must approve any treaty agreed to by the president before it can take effect.

- **War** The president can conduct a war. Only Congress, however, can declare a war. The president commands the armed forces, but Congress controls the money needed to support the armed forces.

- **Veto** The president has the power to veto a bill. Congress has the power to approve the same bill in spite of the president's veto, if two-thirds of each house agree.

How can Congress limit the powers of the president?

- **Impeachment** To impeach means to charge a public official with wrongdoing in office. It also means to bring the official to trial. The House of Representatives has the power to impeach the president. If tried and found guilty by the Senate, the president can be removed from office. Article II of the Constitution says that the president can be removed from office only for "Treason, Bribery, or other high Crimes and Misdemeanors."

In the next lesson, you will learn how the Supreme Court checks the power of the president.

Why do you think departments were created to help the president?

How is the executive branch organized?

George Washington was elected the first president of the United States. The Framers knew that the president would need help in running the executive branch. But, the Framers did not have a plan. The Constitution does not say how the executive branch should be organized. Instead, the Framers left it up to President Washington and Congress to decide how to organize the executive branch.

Washington and Congress worked together to decide what advisors the president would need. Congress created four departments to help the president.

- **Department of State** to handle relations with other countries
- **Department of the Treasury** to handle the money of the federal government
- **Department of War**, now called the Department of Defense, to handle the defense of the nation
- **Attorney General**, now the head of the Department of Justice, to be the chief law enforcement officer

The people in charge of these departments act as advisers to the president. These advisers became known as the president's cabinet. The cabinet now includes the vice president and the heads of fifteen executive departments.

Reviewing and Using the Lesson

1. Explain the process for selecting a president.
2. What are some duties and powers of the president of the United States?
3. Explain four ways that Congress can check the power of the president.
4. What does the president's cabinet do?
5. Who holds each of these offices in the United States today: the president, the vice president, the secretary of state, the secretary of the treasury, the secretary of defense, and the attorney general?

Activities

1. What are the qualifications for being president of the United States? To answer this question, see the Constitution, Article II, Section 1.
2. Article I, Section 1, says that the president is to be elected by "electors" appointed in each state. How many electors does your state have? How are they chosen? Find more information about the process for electing the president. Share what you learn with the class.
3. Today there are fifteen members of the president's cabinet. Find the names of the fifteen cabinet offices. Create a chart that shows the president's cabinet. On the chart, explain what each member does.
4. Find newspaper articles about a duty the president is carrying out. Be prepared to share the articles with your class. Use the articles to create a class bulletin board.
5. Find newspaper articles about Congress or the Supreme Court checking something the president wants to do. Write a report that explains what is happening. Use quotes from the article. Present the report to the class.
6. When in our history did the candidate who won the popular vote not win the Electoral College vote?

LESSON

15

What is the judicial branch?

LESSON PURPOSE

The judicial branch is the system of courts of law. The courts decide what laws mean and settle disagreements about them. In this lesson, you will learn about the duties and powers of the judicial branch. You will learn how this branch is organized.

LESSON OBJECTIVES

When you have finished this lesson, you should be able to

- ❑ describe how the judicial branch is organized,
- ❑ identify some of its powers, and
- ❑ explain some of the limits on its powers.

TERMS TO KNOW

- appeal
- Article III
- associate
- federal courts
- interpret
- judicial review

What does the United States Supreme Court do?

What does the judicial branch do?

The role of the courts is to interpret the law. To **interpret** is to decide the meaning of the law and the Constitution.

The courts settle conflicts between individuals and between the states. The courts also decide if someone is guilty of breaking the law. The courts are responsible for deciding how a guilty person should be punished.

The **federal courts** are the courts of the national government. The federal courts deal with problems between states. Federal courts also handle cases that deal with the Constitution and the laws made by Congress.

How is the judicial branch organized?

The judicial branch of the national government is composed of lower courts and the Supreme Court of the United States. The Supreme Court is the highest court of our national government. We call the nine judges on the Supreme Court *justices*. The head of the Supreme Court is the Chief Justice of the United States. **Article III** of the Constitution describes the responsibilities and powers of this branch.

How are judges in the federal courts selected?

The Framers believed that if the people elected federal judges, the judges might not make fair decisions. They might favor the people who voted for them. For this reason, federal judges are appointed to office. The president appoints all the judges in the federal courts. The Senate must approve each appointment.

Federal judges usually serve in office until they retire or die. Congress has the power to remove federal judges if they are found guilty of serious crimes.

What Do You Think?

What could you do if the government took away some of your rights?

Suppose you thought that one of your rights guaranteed by the Constitution was being abused by government officials. What could you do about it? In what ways might the courts help protect your rights?

What is the power of judicial review?

Judicial review is one of the most important powers of the judicial branch. **Judicial review** is the power of the courts to decide whether the United States Constitution allows a certain law or action of government. Judicial review gives the federal courts the power to

- declare that a law made by Congress is not constitutional,
- declare that an action taken by the president is not constitutional, and
- declare a state law unconstitutional if it conflicts with the laws made by Congress or with the Constitution.

Suppose Congress passed a law that said you must practice a certain religion. The Constitution says Congress cannot do this. You could go to federal court and say that Congress has no right to tell you to belong to a certain religion. The court would review your case. The court has the power to say that the law made by Congress is unconstitutional. If the court does this, the law would not be enforced.

How does the United States Supreme Court check the powers of Congress?

How is the idea of judicial review related to the idea of separation of powers and checks and balances?

What are the limits on the power of the federal courts?

The Constitution says that judges shall hold their offices "during good behavior." Congress has the power to impeach, try, and remove judges from office.

The Constitution does not give the courts the power to enforce their decisions. The president is responsible for enforcing the decisions of the courts.

The Constitution also says that judges' salaries cannot be reduced during their time in office. This means that they cannot be punished for the decisions they make.

What Do You Think?

How would you decide this case?

Suppose that you are a justice of the United States Supreme Court. This case has come to you on appeal from a lower court. **Appeal** means to request that a case from a lower court be heard again. Work in a group of five students. First, read the case. Then, consider the arguments made by both sides. When you finish, the group should decide how it would rule. Not every member of the group has to agree with the decision. The members who agree should write their ideas on a sheet of paper. The members who disagree should do the same. Be prepared to share your decision with the class.

Chicago v. Morales

Police may not arrest people until they commit a crime. In Chicago, the city government was trying to deal with an increase in gang activity. To help the police, the city government passed a law. The new law made loitering by gang members a crime. The law stated that loitering meant, "to remain in one place with no apparent purpose."

If a police officer saw two or more people loitering, the officer was to order them to move away from the area. Anyone who did not move was in violation of the city law. The person could be put in jail for up to six months. The

Do you think that laws against loitering violate a person's rights? Why?

What issues should the court consider in this case?

person might also have to pay a fine or do community service. A person who was able to prove that he or she was not a gang member was to be set free.

A police officer saw Jesús Morales standing with six other people who might be gang members. The officer ordered them all to move on. When the officer came back a little later, the people were still there. The officer then arrested them.

Jesús Morales took his case to the state courts. He claimed that the law violated his rights to move about freely and to associate with others. To **associate** means to join with others as a partner, member, or friend. Morales also argued that the law was unfair. It punished people not for what they have done but for who they are. The state courts ruled in favor of Morales.

The city of Chicago took the case to the United States Supreme Court. The city argued that street gangs scare people, and they make the community unsafe. Giving the police power to arrest loitering gang members helps to prevent crime. The law, the city said, does not violate the right to associate with others. It is directed only at loitering. Otherwise, people may associate with whomever they want.

In this case, the Supreme Court has to weigh the rights of individuals against the need of the city to prevent crime. If you were a member of the Supreme Court, how would you decide this case?

Reviewing and Using the Lesson

1. What is the role of the judicial branch of our government?
2. What is the highest court in the judicial branch?
3. Why are Supreme Court justices and other federal judges appointed and not elected?
4. What is judicial review? Why is it one of the most important powers of the judicial branch?

Activities

1. Find a recent article in a newspaper that discusses a case the Supreme Court is hearing. Be prepared to explain the article to your class.
2. With your teacher's help, invite an attorney or a judge to come to your classroom. Ask her or him to discuss how our court system works. Prepare your questions before the guest's visit.
3. Learn the names of and something about the current United States Supreme Court justices or some famous justices of the past.

LESSON 16

How did the Constitution create a federal system of government?

LESSON PURPOSE

The Constitution created a new system of government. We call it a federal system. In this lesson, you will learn what a federal system is and how it works. You will learn how power is delegated to the national and state governments. You also will learn which powers both governments share.

LESSON OBJECTIVES

When you have finished this lesson, you should be able to

- ❑ describe our federal system,
- ❑ explain some of the powers that are given to our national and state governments, and
- ❑ explain some of the limits on the powers of our national and state governments.

TERMS TO KNOW

- delegate
- federal government
- federal system
- supremacy
- supremacy clause

What powers should be shared by the national and state governments? Why?

What new system of government did the Framers create?

When the Framers wrote our Constitution, they created a **federal system** of government. Our national government is also called the **federal government**. In our federal system, the powers of our national and state governments come from the people.

"We the People" delegate some powers to our national government. To **delegate** means to entrust to someone else. We delegate some powers to our state governments. We delegate some powers to be shared by both the national and state governments. Finally, we keep some powers for ourselves.

Critical Thinking Exercise

What is a federal system?

With a partner, look at the illustration below. It shows how our federal system of government works. Then, answer the questions and be prepared to share your answers with the class.

1. Where does power come from in our federal system of government?
2. To whom is power delegated?
3. Why do you think the Framers chose a federal system of government?
4. What are some advantages of a federal system of government? What might be some disadvantages?

In a federal system, how do the people delegate their power?

Why do you think state governments have the power to create public schools?

How have the people delegated power?

Here are some examples of how the people delegate power in our federal system.

Powers to the national government

We give some powers to our national government. These include the power to

- tax the people to support the national government,
- declare and conduct war,
- control trade between the states and with other nations,
- create post offices, and
- coin money.

Powers to the state governments

We give some powers to our state governments. These include the power to

- tax the people to support the state government,
- create public schools,
- control trade within the state,
- make motor vehicle and traffic laws, and
- make laws regulating marriage and divorce.

Powers the national and state governments share

The national and state governments share certain powers. These include power to

- tax the people,
- borrow money,
- provide for the health and welfare of the people,
- make laws, and
- create a court system.

Powers kept by the people

We keep certain powers and rights for ourselves. These include the right to

- practice our religious beliefs or not hold any religious beliefs,
- express our opinions in speech or writing or by other peaceable means, and
- join with others to ask our government to do or not do certain things.

Which level of government has the most power?

The Constitution says, "This Constitution, and the laws of the United States … shall be the supreme law of the land." We call this the supremacy clause. **Supremacy** means to be highest in rank. The **supremacy clause** says that the states cannot make laws that are in conflict with the United States Constitution. States also cannot make laws that are in conflict with the laws made by Congress.

What does this illustration tell you about the supremacy clause?

Pennsylvania governor Tom Wolf signs a bill into law. What are some limits on the powers of state governments?

What limits does the Constitution place upon national and state governments?

A constitutional government means that the powers of government are limited. The Constitution limits the powers of both the national and state governments.

Limits on the powers of the national government

These are some examples of limits on the powers of the national government. The national government may not

- make laws that favor trade in one state over the others,
- spend money unless there is a law giving it approval to do so, or
- tax goods that are leaving the country.

Limits on the powers of the state governments

These are some examples of limits on the powers of the state government. The state governments may not

- coin or print money,

- engage in war unless actually invaded or in immediate danger of being invaded, or

- make treaties with other nations.

Limits on both national and state governments

These are some examples of limits on the powers of both the national and state governments. They may not

- deny people the right to freedom of religion and expression,

- deny people the equal protection of the laws, or

- deny a trial by jury to those accused of a crime.

Is the way the Constitution organizes and limits powers enough to protect our rights?

You now understand something about how the Framers wrote the Constitution to organize our government. We have a national or federal government. We have state governments, and we have local governments in our towns and cities.

Many Framers believed this way of organizing our government was enough to protect our rights. Some Americans were worried that the new Constitution gave too much power to the national government. They refused to accept the Constitution unless a bill of rights was added to it.

What rights are the state and national governments not allowed to deny?

Reviewing and Using the Lesson

1. Where does our government get its powers?
2. Explain how our federal system of government works.
3. What are some powers that the Constitution grants to the national government?
4. What are some powers that the Constitution grants to the states?
5. What are some powers that the national and state governments share?
6. What are some examples of rights that the people kept for themselves?
7. What are some limits on the powers of the national government?
8. What are some limits on the powers of the state governments?
9. What is the supremacy clause?

Activities

1. Make a chart that shows what might happen if a state violates the supremacy clause.
2. Draw your own picture or cartoon that shows how our federal system of government works.
3. Use the internet. Look for newspapers from different states. Find examples of the use of power by federal, state, and local governments. Be prepared to explain the examples to your class.

UNIT
4

How does the Constitution protect our basic rights?

UNIT 4

How does the Constitution protect our basic rights?

Many Founders were worried that the rights of the people were not well protected by the new Constitution. They said they would not help to get the Constitution approved unless a bill of rights was added. The other Founders agreed to add one when the first Congress met, and that is exactly what happened.

The Bill of Rights is the name of the first ten amendments to the Constitution. This part of the Constitution was added in 1791. Since that time, other amendments have been added. Many of the amendments give rights to people who were not given these rights in the original Constitution. For example, the Nineteenth Amendment, added in 1920, gave women the right to vote.

KEY TOPICS

- Bill of Rights
- due process of law
- equal protection of the laws
- freedom of expression
- freedom of religion
- right to vote

LESSON 17

How does the Constitution protect your right to freedom of expression?

LESSON PURPOSE

The Founders believed that freedom of expression is important for all citizens. In this lesson, you will learn the meaning of freedom of expression. You will learn why freedom of expression is important to you and to our nation. You will also learn about when it might be reasonable to limit this freedom.

LESSON OBJECTIVES

When you have finished this lesson, you should be able to

- ❑ explain what freedom of expression means,
- ❑ list some of the benefits of freedom of expression, and
- ❑ describe situations in which it is fair and reasonable to limit your right to freedom of expression.

TERMS TO KNOW

- assembly
- defamation
- expression
- freedom of expression
- petition
- press
- speech

What is a petition? How is signing a petition a form of expression?

What is freedom of expression?

Suppose someone asked you to name the freedoms that you think are very important. Most Americans would say that it is important to have these freedoms:

- **Speech** The right to talk about your beliefs, ideas, or feelings
- **Press** The right to read and write whatever you wish
- **Assembly** The right to meet with others to discuss your beliefs, ideas, or feelings
- **Petition** The right to ask your government to correct things that you think are wrong or to do things you believe are needed

The rights to freedom of **speech**, **press**, **assembly**, and **petition** are all a part of **freedom of expression**. **Expression** means to communicate your beliefs, ideas, or feelings to others. The First Amendment of the Bill of Rights protects our right to freedom of expression.

Our Constitution limits the powers of our government in order to protect these freedoms. Under our Constitution, the government cannot interfere with these rights except under very special circumstances.

What are the benefits of freedom of expression?

Freedom of expression is important to all people who live in a democracy.

Freedom of expression supports our democracy

Our democratic system of government depends on the people's ability to make good decisions. To make good decisions, you need to be able to get enough information to make up your mind. You need to hear and discuss different ideas and opinions. Discussing different points of view will help you in many ways. You can make reasonable choices about supporting leaders. You also will know which laws deserve your support.

Freedom of expression helps us grow as individuals

When you express your thoughts and listen to the ideas of others, you learn and become more mature. Hearing and discussing different points of view helps you make thoughtful choices about what you think is right. You mature as a person when you make choices for yourself rather than just accepting what others tell you.

Why is freedom of the press so important?

What benefits do individuals and society gain from the right to freedom of expression?

Freedom of expression advances knowledge

It is easier for you to make new discoveries and gain new knowledge when you can suggest ideas and exchange information freely. Even if some ideas do not work, they provide a way of testing the truth of other ideas.

Freedom of expression makes peaceful change in society possible

If you are free to try to persuade others to change things, you are less likely to use violence. We have improved many things in our country by using our right to freedom of expression. If we may criticize things we cannot change, we may be willing to have patience until we can get them changed.

Why was freedom of expression important to the Founders?

The Founders of our nation knew it was necessary to protect freedom of expression. Throughout history, governments had often tried to stop people from spreading new ideas or criticizing government actions.

Some people in the American colonies had suffered—and in some cases died—for expressing their ideas. Three examples are Mary Dyer, John Buckner, and John Peter Zenger.

Mary Dyer lived in Massachusetts. In 1660, the Puritan leaders had her put to death. The Puritans said that she taught people that slavery, war, and the death penalty were wrong.

John Buckner was a printer in Virginia. In 1682, he used his press to print the laws of the colony. The governor of Virginia said that Buckner did not have permission to print the laws. He banned all printing presses in the colony. The governor said, "Printing has encouraged [the people] to learn and even criticize the best government. God, keep us from free schools and printing."

John Peter Zenger was a newspaperman in New York. In 1735, he published an article criticizing the royal governor. At that time, it was against the law to criticize the government. The governor had Zenger arrested and thrown in jail. After a long trial, Zenger was set free even though he had broken the law. The jury decided that what Zenger had said was true. They decided he should not be punished for telling the truth even though it was against the law to do so.

These are some reasons why the Founders and others believed it was necessary to protect freedom of expression. It is why they insisted that this protection be in the Constitution.

When is it fair and reasonable to limit free expression?

This is such an important freedom that it is not easy to answer the question. Over the years, the courts have given us some guidelines. These guidelines help to balance the right to free expression against other important rights and interests of society. Here are some examples of what the courts have said.

- **Imminent threat** Speech may be limited when it is clear that it could lead to immediate violence or a riot. That means the speech must be stopped to protect the public's safety. Speech may also be limited if it is a danger to our national security. This means that you cannot publish or give military secrets to other countries. This would be dangerous for the entire nation.

How did John Peter Zenger's arrest help the Founders decide that freedom of expression is important?

Should people be able to express their ideas loudly even in the middle of the night? Why or why not?

- **Time, place, and manner** Government may make rules saying when, where, and how you may speak. These rules might forbid using a loudspeaker in a residential neighborhood in the middle of the night. The rules might require that you get a permit to march in the streets to protest a government action.

  These rules, however, may not regulate what you want to say. The rules may not make it difficult or impossible for you to express your ideas to others. Nor may they favor one point of view over another. This means that government may not give a permit to conduct a rally to a group whose ideas it favors and deny the same right to a group it does not.

- **Defamation** Purposely saying or writing false information about a person or group that seriously injures their reputation is called **defamation**. Government may make laws punishing people for defaming other people or groups.

What Do You Think?

When are other rights and interests more important than freedom of expression?

Freedom of expression is so important that it is not easy to answer this question. Discuss the situations below. You will discover other important rights and interests of society. These other rights and interests must be balanced with our right to freedom of expression.

Work with a partner or in small groups. Read all the situations or the ones assigned to your group. Then answer the three questions about the situations you have read. Be prepared to share your group's ideas with the class.

1. What rights and interests might be endangered in this situation?
2. Should this kind of expression be limited? Why?
3. What rule can you make to limit this kind of expression?

- You learn some of our nation's military secrets. Should you be able to sell the secrets to another country?
- People are very angry about the results of a trial in your community. You want to stand in front of the crowd and shout, "Let's go and shut down the courthouse right now!"
- You are thinking about telling lies in a court of law to protect your friend.
- You want to use a loudspeaker in the middle of the night in your quiet neighborhood.
- A parent goes into a kindergarten class and starts swearing.
- You think that someone you work with is a bad person. So, you tell lies about her that harm her reputation. You cause her to lose her job.

Critical Thinking Exercise

Should freedom of expression be limited in this case?

Suppose you are a justice of the United States Supreme Court. Read the case below. Then work with a group of five students. Read and discuss the opinions that follow the case. Decide which opinion you would agree with or develop your own opinion. Be prepared to explain your reasons to the class.

Feiner v. New York (1951)

On the evening of March 8, college student Irving Feiner stood on a wooden box on a street corner in Syracuse, New York. He was addressing a racially mixed crowd of about seventy-five people. The police received a telephone call about the meeting, and two police officers were sent to find out what was happening.

Feiner urged the African Americans in the crowd to take up arms and fight for equal rights. He urged them to attend a meeting later that night to talk about equal rights. Feiner told the crowd that the president of the United States, the mayor of the city, and other public officials were bums. His words gave the impression that he was trying to get the people to become violent and to fight for their rights.

The crowd became restless. Feelings both for and against the speaker were rising. For thirty minutes, the police made no effort to interfere with the speech, but they were concerned about the crowd. There was some pushing and shoving, and as Feiner continued to speak, one man threatened him with violence.

The officers asked Feiner three times to get off the box. Then they demanded that Feiner stop talking. Finally, the officers arrested Feiner and charged him with disorderly conduct. This law makes it a crime to encourage people to use violence. The officers said that they had acted to control the crowd, to keep the peace, and to prevent injury.

At his trial, the state court found Feiner guilty and sentenced him to prison. Feiner appealed the decision. Feiner said that the police were trying to silence his views in violation of his right to freedom of speech.

Do you think Feiner's speech was a lawful speech? Did it go beyond persuasion, and did he try to encourage a riot? Did the police violate Feiner's right of free speech?

Opinion 1: The police did not violate Feiner's right of free speech

The officers making the arrest were responsible for keeping law and order. They were not trying to keep Feiner from expressing his views and opinions. The way Feiner acted and the immediate danger of the audience becoming violent were reasons enough for the police to arrest him. Freedom of speech does not include the right to try to make people use violence or to riot.

Opinion 2: The police did violate Feiner's right of free speech

The facts do not show any immediate danger of a riot or disorder. It is not unusual that some people at public street meetings push, shove, or disagree with the speaker. The police had a duty to protect Feiner's right to speak. The crowd was restless, but the police did not try to quiet it. One man threatened Feiner, but the officers did nothing to discourage this man. Instead, the police acted only to stop Feiner's speech.

When do you think the government should have the power to limit your right to freedom of expression?

Reviewing and Using the Lesson

1. What are the four types of free expression? Give examples of each. Where in the Constitution will you find the right to freedom of expression?
2. Why did the Founders believe it is important to protect free expression?
3. List four benefits of freedom of expression. Give examples of each. Which do you think is most important? Why?
4. In what kinds of situations do you think it is fair and reasonable to limit freedom of expression? Give examples.

Activities

1. Learn about the policies in your school district or the rules at your school that regulate how students may exercise freedom of expression. Share what you learned with the class.
2. Make a poster that shows the four parts of freedom of expression. In your poster, show people exercising these rights. Share your poster with the class.
3. Imagine that a group with unpopular opinions wants to hold a meeting at a public park in your community. Most of the people in your community do not agree with the views of this group. The people fear that the meeting might become disorderly and disturb the peace. Work with a partner. One of you should prepare a discussion in favor of allowing the group to hold the meeting. The other should prepare a discussion against allowing the group to hold the meeting. Both of you should present your opinions to the class and then let the class decide.
4. Find a newspaper article that shows someone exercising the right to freedom of expression. Write a short essay that explains the benefits of this right to you and your community.

LESSON 18

How does the Constitution protect your right to freedom of religion?

LESSON PURPOSE

The Founders thought the right to freedom of religion was so important that they placed it at the beginning of the Bill of Rights. In this lesson, you will learn why the Founders thought this freedom was so important. You will learn how the Constitution protects religious freedom. You will also study situations in which religious freedom may be limited when it conflicts with other important rights and interests.

LESSON OBJECTIVES

When you have finished this lesson, you should be able to

- ❑ explain the importance of freedom of religion and
- ❑ explain when it might be reasonable to limit this freedom.

TERMS TO KNOW

- discriminate
- establishment clause
- free exercise clause
- freedom of belief or conscience
- tolerant

Why did the Founders think that freedom of religion needed to be protected in the Bill of Rights?

How does the First Amendment protect freedom of religion?

The first words of the Bill of Rights protect your right to freedom of religion. They say, "Congress shall make no law respecting [about] an establishment of religion, or prohibiting the free exercise thereof." These words show how important freedom of religion was to the Founders. Here is what these words mean.

- Congress may not establish (set up) an official religion for our country or favor any one religion over others. This is the **establishment clause**.

- Congress may not stop you from holding any religious beliefs you choose or from having no religious beliefs at all. The government may not unfairly or unreasonably limit your right to practice any religious beliefs you wish. This is the **free exercise clause**.

Why was freedom of religion so important to the colonists?

Many colonists came from Europe to the New World in search of religious freedom. Two such groups were the Puritans and the Pilgrims. They controlled the government and the religious practices of the Massachusetts Bay Colony.

Those who disagreed with the beliefs of the Puritans were sometimes persecuted or even executed. Others, such as the Puritan minister Roger Williams, were forced to leave the colony.

Roger Williams and his wife Mary believed that the church and the government should be separate. Williams wanted the church to be tolerant of the beliefs of others. To be **tolerant** means being willing to let other people hold opinions that are different from your own. These ideas angered the Puritan leaders. So, they forced Roger and Mary Williams and their followers to leave. The group left and founded the colony of Rhode Island.

By the end of the American Revolution, there were people of many different religions in America. There were Baptists, Catholics, Jews, and Quakers, for example. All believed they had as much right as anyone else to practice their religions. As a result, Americans got used to living with people of different religious beliefs. People began to believe that others should have the same rights they wanted for themselves.

What religious conflicts did the colonists have before the Constitution was written?

Why was freedom of religion so important to the Founders?

Leaders such as Thomas Jefferson and James Madison thought it was unfair to discriminate against people because of their religious beliefs. To **discriminate** against people means to treat them unfairly. They thought such discrimination took away the rights of the people and was dangerous to the common good.

Most of the Founders were religious men and women. They did not want government to interfere with the right of the people to practice their religion. George Washington believed that people needed religion to develop good character. He did not believe in using taxes, however, to pay for teaching religion in public schools. The Founders' strong belief in religious freedom led them to protect it first and foremost in the First Amendment.

Can government limit your right to freedom of belief?

You may believe in any religion you wish or in no religion at all. This is stated in the free exercise clause. You have the right to **freedom of belief or conscience**. The government may not force you to swear to a belief you do not hold. You may not be forced by the government to pray in school or any other place.

Can government put limits on how you practice your beliefs?

The free exercise clause protects your right to practice your beliefs. But, this right may be limited. Not everyone agrees with all the limitations placed upon religious practices. You will often hear differences of opinion about this subject.

Should government tell you what religious beliefs you must have or how to practice your religion? Why or why not?

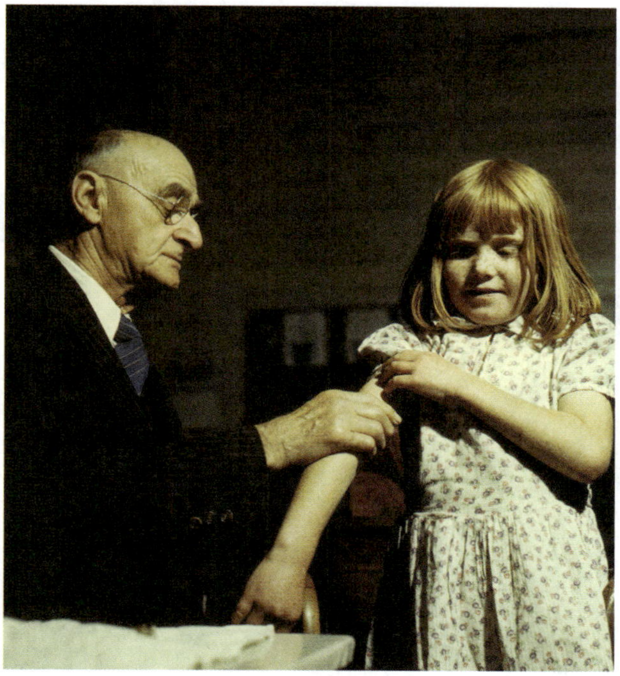

Why are some religious practices, such as the refusal to get vaccinations or the refusal to use road reflectors, not protected by the Constitution?

Your religious practices may only be limited if they are considered harmful to public health or the common good. Suppose your religion forbids vaccination. The public authorities may still require anyone who attends school to get a vaccination. Vaccination is required for the protection of the common good. Other religious practices, such as handling snakes, refusing to use modern reflectors required for road safety, and parents refusing medical care for their children, are all issues that have gone to the courts.

In our country, people have the right to hold different opinions. They have the right to try to get laws changed to protect their particular religious practices. They also have the right to argue their positions in our courts.

What is the conflict about establishment of religion?

At the time the Constitution was written, almost every nation in Europe had one official religion. People who did not want to belong to that religion were often denied certain rights. They could not attend some schools or hold a government office. They were often discriminated against or persecuted just because they did not belong to the official religion of the government.

When a government only supports one official religion, we say that it is the established religion of the government. The First Amendment does not allow our government to have an established religion or to favor one religion over others.

Do you think public schools should be allowed to set aside time for prayer? Why or why not?

There are often conflicts, however, about what the establishment clause means. Most conflicts about the establishment clause have been about religion in public schools. Does the establishment clause mean that public schools may not have prayers in the classroom? Does it mean that government may not give money to religious schools to buy textbooks? These are not easy questions to answer. Many cases about religion and the public schools have gone to the United States Supreme Court.

What Do You Think?

How would you decide this case?

Read about the court case *Engle v. Vitale*. Then, in small groups discuss the questions that follow it. Be prepared to share your ideas with the class.

Engle v. Vitale (1962)

In 1958, a board of education in New York gave the district's principals a prayer to be recited in their schools. Teachers were required to lead students in saying the prayer aloud every day. Students who did not want to say the prayer were permitted to sit quietly or leave the room.

The parents of ten students complained. They said the use of this prayer in public schools was against their religious beliefs. They said that praying was something people should do at home and in church. They also said that to have prayers in school put pressure on all students to say the prayer. Students who did not want to say the prayer might be criticized. The parents took the case to court.

1. Suppose your teacher began each day by leading the class in saying a prayer. Would this violate your right to believe in any religion you wish or to believe in no religion at all? Why or why not?

2. Teachers in this school system were paid by tax money collected from the citizens of New York. Does this mean that the government was supporting religion? Why or why not?

3. Do you think it is all right for the government to support religion if it helps all religions equally? Why or why not?

4. Do you think the Board of Education violated the Constitution? Why or why not?

Reviewing and Using the Lesson

1. In what part of the Constitution will you find the right to freedom of religion?
2. What is the meaning of the establishment clause?
3. What is the meaning of the free exercise clause?
4. Freedom of belief is an absolute right. What does this mean?
5. Can you think of any situations when the government would have a duty to restrict religious practices?

Activities

1. What religious beliefs did Native Americans in the colonies have? What religious beliefs did African Americans in the colonies have? What were their ideas about freedom of religion? Share what you learn in the form of a report, a poem, or a song.
2. Learn about different religious beliefs held in the colonies by European Americans: Baptists, Catholics, Jews, Puritans, or Quakers. What were their ideas about freedom of religion? Write a newspaper article about one or more of these groups to share with the class.
3. Thomas Jefferson and James Madison had strong opinions about the separation of church and state. Find out what they said about freedom of religion. Write a short story about what they would say about these issues today.
4. Draw a picture expressing your opinion of the *Engle v. Vitale* case.

LESSON 19

How does the Constitution protect your right to equal protection of the laws?

LESSON PURPOSE

In this lesson, you will learn about the right of all people to be treated equally by government. You will learn the meaning of the term *equal protection of the laws*. The equal protection clause is one part of the Fourteenth Amendment. This clause has been used to prevent states from being unfair to citizens because of their race or gender.

LESSON OBJECTIVES

When you have finished this lesson, you should be able to

- ❑ explain the meaning of equal protection of the laws and
- ❑ describe some important steps in history that were taken to prevent state governments from being unfair to people.

TERMS TO KNOW

- boycott
- Civil Rights Act of 1964
- Civil War Amendments
- equal protection clause
- equal protection of the laws
- segregate
- Voting Rights Act

Critical Thinking Exercise

Are these actions by government fair?

Work in a group of three to five students. Discuss each of the imaginary situations below. Decide if the government was being fair in the situation. Be prepared to share the reasons for your decisions with the class.

1. A new law in your state says that you must go to a certain school because of your race.
2. Your town has a law that says that you cannot live in a certain area because of your religion.
3. Your city police department will not allow women on the police force.
4. Your state has a law that says you cannot marry someone of a different race.
5. A man and a woman work for the state government at the same jobs. The man is paid much more than the woman is paid.

Why is it important that government not restrict a person's choice of a job?

Why was the Fourteenth Amendment needed?

After the Civil War, three amendments were added to the Constitution: the Thirteenth, Fourteenth, and Fifteenth Amendments. We call these the **Civil War Amendments**. They ended slavery and attempted to give former slaves the same rights as other people.

The Fourteenth Amendment was passed to stop state governments from unfairly discriminating against African Americans. To unfairly discriminate means to treat some people differently without having a good reason. The Fourteenth Amendment says, "No State shall ... deny to any person ... the equal protection of the laws." **Equal protection of the laws** means that state governments must not treat people differently unless there is a good and fair reason for doing so.

There are good and fair reasons why most states have laws that say you cannot drive a car until you are a certain age. The **equal protection clause** prohibits laws that unreasonably and unfairly favor some groups over others.

Just passing the Civil War Amendments in 1868 did not stop unfair treatment of African Americans. States still passed laws that allowed unfair discrimination. Some states passed laws that

Why did the Civil War Amendments fail to end the unfair treatment of African Americans by government?

required African American children to go to schools separate from other children. Other laws required separate seats on trains and separate entrances to buildings. Some laws made it impossible for African Americans to vote or have the basic rights that other citizens had.

These state laws were unfair. People said they violated the Fourteenth Amendment. In 1896, the Supreme Court ruled that laws requiring separation of the races were constitutional. The Court said it was legal for states to separate people by race if the public places for each group were equal. For example, separate schools should have the same quality of classrooms and teachers.

During the next half century, Americans' ideas about fairness and equality began to change. In 1954, the Supreme Court decided one of the most important legal cases in our country's history.

What is the importance of *Brown v. Board of Education*?

Linda Brown was a seven-year-old African American student. She lived in Topeka, Kansas. Her home was five blocks from an elementary school. The school close to Linda's home was for white students only. The school board required that Linda cross town to go to a school twenty-one blocks away. The school that was far away was for African American students.

Linda's parents sued the school board of Topeka. They said that the school system was treating Linda unfairly. They claimed that the school board had violated Linda's right to the equal protection of the laws.

How did Thurgood Marshall help bring an end to segregation in our country?

One of the Brown's lawyers was Thurgood Marshall. Marshall later became the first African American justice of the Supreme Court. He argued that segregated schools could not be equal. To **segregate** means to set apart from others. The Supreme Court agreed. The Court said that segregated schools by their nature were not equal. The Court said that requiring separate schools denied students the equal protection of the laws.

How did people work to change the laws and end unfair discrimination?

The *Brown* case dealt only with public schools. It did not end other types of unfair discrimination. The civil rights movement started in the 1950s. It was a time when many people of both races worked to end other kinds of unfair treatment. The people marched in the streets. They wrote letters to Congress asking for stronger laws. They held boycotts. A **boycott** is an act of protest. It means that, as a group, people avoid something like a store or company.

One of the earliest boycotts began in 1955. Rosa Parks was a working woman who lived in Alabama. On her way home one day, Parks refused to give her seat on the bus to a white person. Parks was arrested for violating a city law. The African American community boycotted the city buses until the city changed the law. The boycott lasted more than a year.

How did people involved in the civil rights movement achieve their goals?

In August of 1963, thousands of Americans marched in Washington, D.C. They wanted to show their support for the civil rights movement. Martin Luther King Jr. was an important civil rights leader. It was here that King gave his famous "I Have a Dream" speech. King told the crowd, "I have a dream that my four little children will one day live in a nation where they will not be judged by the color of their skin, but by the content of their character."

In 1964, Congress passed a law called the Civil Rights Act. The **Civil Rights Act of 1964** ended segregation in public places. Public places included restaurants, movie theaters, and hotels. The law also said that employers could not unfairly discriminate against people because of their race, national origin, religion, or gender.

The Civil Rights Act made it against the law to segregate people in public places. It did not stop African Americans and other minorities from being unfairly discriminated against when they tried to vote in elections. So, in 1965 Congress passed the **Voting Rights Act**. It is one of the most important acts ever passed by Congress. It protects the right to vote for members of minority groups that had been discriminated against unfairly since the nation was founded.

How did Martin Luther King Jr. strengthen the civil rights movement?

What were the results of the Civil Rights Act of 1964?

How has the equal protection clause been used to protect the rights of people with disabilities?

How has the equal protection clause helped other groups in America?

As African Americans won the right to equal protection, other groups began to ask for the same right. Asians, Latinos, Native Americans, people with disabilities, the elderly, and other groups have worked to gain the right to equal protection. It is now against the law to unfairly discriminate because of a person's age, disability, or ethnic background.

Women were the largest group to benefit from these efforts. Many laws protect women from unfair discrimination where they work. The law prohibits discrimination in pay based on gender. Education programs that receive money from the federal government cannot discriminate based on gender.

Reviewing and Using the Lesson

1. Why was the Fourteenth Amendment added to the Constitution?
2. What does "equal protection of the laws" mean?
3. Why did the Fourteenth Amendment not immediately end unfair treatment of African Americans?
4. Why was the *Brown v. Board of Education* legal case so important?
5. What was the civil rights movement? Give some examples of how people of different races worked together to change unfair laws.
6. Why was the Civil Rights Act of 1964 important?
7. Why was the Voting Rights Act of 1965 important?

Activities

1. Learn about important people in the civil rights movement: Martin Luther King Jr., Rosa Parks, Linda Brown, and Medgar Evers. Share what you learned with your class.
2. Read Martin Luther King Jr.'s "I Have a Dream" speech. Draw a picture or a poster showing King's dream. Share your picture with the class.
3. Learn more about how one of the following groups struggled to achieve the right to equal protection of the law. Share what you learned with the class.
   - Chinese
   - Latinos
   - Native Americans
   - People with disabilities
   - Women

LESSON 20

How does the Constitution protect your right to due process of law?

LESSON PURPOSE

In this lesson, you will learn another way the Constitution protects your right to be treated fairly by government. You will learn the meaning of the term *due process of law*. You will learn how due process protects you from unfair and unreasonable acts by people in government.

LESSON OBJECTIVES

When you have finished this lesson, you should be able to explain why your right to due process of law is so important.

TERMS TO KNOW

- Fifth Amendment
- Fourteenth Amendment
- right to due process of law

Why is it important that the federal government use fair procedures when it gathers information about people during a census, which is conducted every ten years?

What is the right to due process of law?

The **right to due process of law** is the right to be treated fairly by your government. It means that members of government must use fair methods or procedures when doing their jobs. They must use fair procedures when they gather information. They must use fair procedures when they use information they have gathered to make decisions.

You will find the term *due process of law* used in two places in the United States Constitution.

- **Fifth Amendment** It says that no person shall be "deprived of [have taken away] life, liberty, or property without due process of law."

  The **Fifth Amendment** protects your right to be treated fairly by the *federal* government.

- **Fourteenth Amendment** It says "nor shall any State deprive any person of life, liberty, or property without due process of law."

  The **Fourteenth Amendment** protects your right to be treated fairly by your *state* and *local* governments.

The Bill of Rights only protects you from unfair treatment by the federal government. The Fourteenth Amendment protects you from unfair treatment by state and local governments.

Why are due process rights important in your daily life?

You have the right to be treated fairly by all agencies of your government. For example, the government must treat you fairly whenever it creates laws about your right to travel, raise a family, use your property, or receive an education and other government benefits. It also means that government must treat you fairly when it enforces the law and settles disagreements about the law in courts. Due process also requires that people in government follow the law.

What Do You Think?

Why is due process important in criminal trials?

It is very important that you understand the meaning of fair procedures in enforcing the law. Read the following imaginary situations. Use the questions to help you explain what is wrong in each situation.

- The police suspect you of a crime. Suppose they use force to make you give them information to show that you might be guilty.
- You must appear in court. Suppose the judge listens to all the witnesses against you but does not allow you to present your side of the story.
- The leaders of the country make decisions about your life, liberty, and property. Suppose they make these decisions in secret. They do not allow you or anyone else to participate.

1. Do you believe that you would be treated fairly if you were accused of a crime? Why or why not?
2. Even if you have not broken the law or been arrested, would you want other people suspected of crimes treated in these ways? Why or why not?
3. Would you want decisions that affected your life, liberty, or property made in secret? Why or why not?

What might happen to people accused of crimes if there were no right to due process of law?

Critical Thinking Exercise

Why should you have the right to a lawyer?

The Bill of Rights says that if you are accused of a crime, you have the right to have a lawyer defend you. Suppose the government did not allow you to have a lawyer. The government would have violated your right to due process, which is guaranteed by the Constitution.

- What does the right to have a lawyer in a criminal case mean?
- Must the government pay a lawyer to defend you if you cannot afford to pay for one yourself?

In the famous case, *Gideon v. Wainwright*, the United States Supreme Court thought again about what the constitutional right to a lawyer means. In a small group, read the following story. Then answer the questions that follow it. Be prepared to share your responses with the class.

Gideon v. Wainwright (1963)

The police accused Clarence Gideon of breaking into a poolroom in Florida. They said he had stolen a pint of wine and taken some coins from a cigarette machine. Gideon was fifty years old. He was a poor, uneducated man who did not know much about the law.

Do you think it is important to have a lawyer defend you in a court of law? Why?

In court, Gideon asked the judge to appoint a lawyer for him. Gideon said that he was too poor to hire one himself. The judge said no. He said that Gideon did not have the right to have the court pay for a lawyer. The court could only do so when the charge was murder.

Gideon was tried before a jury. He tried to be his own lawyer. He made an opening speech to the jury. He asked questions of the witnesses against him. Gideon called his own witnesses to tell his side of the story. Then he made his final speech to the jury.

The jury decided that Gideon was guilty of the charges. The judge sent Gideon to prison for five years.

While in prison, Gideon wrote a petition to the Supreme Court. He wrote it by hand and in pencil. Gideon argued that all citizens have a right to a lawyer in cases where they might be sent to prison. The Court agreed to hear the appeal.

1. Should the judge have appointed a lawyer to help Gideon? Why or why not?

2. Should the right to have a lawyer mean that government has to provide one for all people who do not have the money to hire one? Why or why not?

3. When should a person have a right to a lawyer?

   - Upon arrest?
   - Before being questioned?
   - Before the trial?
   - After the trial, if the person thinks the trial was unfair and wants another trial?

What right did Gideon exercise while in prison? Why is this right important?

Reviewing and Using the Lesson

1. What does the right to due process mean?

2. Why is the right to due process important?

3. Explain how due process protects your right to life, liberty, and property from unfair and unreasonable acts by people in government.

4. How does the Fourteenth Amendment differ from the Fifth Amendment in what it says about due process?

Activities

1. Watch a television drama or movie that deals with law enforcement. Keep a journal of how due process rights are protected or violated. Share your observations with the class.

2. With your teacher's help, invite a police officer to your class. Ask the officer to discuss what the police have to do to protect due process rights when they suspect someone of a crime. Prepare questions to ask your guest before the visit.

3. Find a newspaper article that gives an example of a due process right. Share your article with the class.

4. Draw a picture or poster. Divide your poster into two parts. On one side, show a situation in which a due process right is being violated. On the other side, show the same situation but with the due process right being protected. Share your drawing with the class.

5. Interview your school principal or a school board member. Ask them about your school's due process rules when dealing with students. Share what you learn with your class.

LESSON 21

How does the Constitution protect your right to vote?

LESSON PURPOSE

Today, citizens of the United States who are eighteen years of age or older have the right to vote. It was not always this way. In this lesson, you will learn how people worked to gain the right to vote. You will learn the laws and amendments to the Constitution that give citizens this right.

LESSON OBJECTIVES

When you have finished this lesson, you should be able to explain how people of different groups gained the right to vote.

TERMS TO KNOW

- civil rights movement
- grandfather clause
- literacy test
- Nineteenth Amendment
- poll tax
- Twenty-fourth Amendment
- Twenty-sixth Amendment

What Do You Think?

Should the right to vote be given to all people?

Work in a group of three to five students. Answer these questions. Be prepared to share your opinions with the class.

1. Why should people have the right to vote for or choose government officials in an election?
2. Who should have the right to vote for government officials?
3. Who should not have this right? Explain your reasons.
4. Should all the states have the same rules for allowing people to vote?

How is the right to vote related to the ideas of republican government and consent of the governed?

Why did the states limit the right to vote to white male property owners?

The Framers could not agree about who should have the right to vote. They left it up to the state governments to decide. Early in our nation's history, the state governments usually only allowed white men who owned property to vote. They believed that a white man with property could have a lot to lose if a bad government came to power. Therefore, he would be more careful with his vote. He would choose leaders who would respect his property.

During the fifty years after the adoption of the Constitution, the states gave the right to vote to all white men, not only those who owned property. African Americans, Native Americans, and women still could not vote. It took many years and much hard work before these groups gained the right to vote.

The right to vote in a democracy is very important. It is also a right that many citizens frequently ignore.

In 1776, why were only white men who owned property allowed to vote?

How did African American men gain the right to vote?

More than 130 years ago, the Thirteenth Amendment ended slavery in America. You read about the Civil War Amendments in Lesson 19. They were intended to give the newly freed slaves the rights of citizens.

- The Thirteenth Amendment abolished slavery.
- The Fourteenth Amendment made the newly freed slaves citizens of the United States.
- The Fifteenth Amendment said that states could not deny the right to vote to anyone because of race or color, or because the person had once been a slave.

The Fifteenth Amendment gave African American men the right to vote. Many Southern states, however, passed laws that made it impossible for African Americans to vote. Here are some examples of these laws.

- **Literacy test** A test to prove that a person is able to read and write is called a **literacy test**. Some states required that African American men pass these tests to be able to vote. Most African American men had been denied an education. Often the people who gave the test were unfair. They made it impossible for even educated African American men to pass the test.

Were the Civil War Amendments enough to guarantee the right of African Americans to vote? Why or why not?

In 1963, people from all over the United States marched on Washington, D.C., for civil rights and jobs. What rights were the people who participated in the civil rights movement exercising?

- **Grandfather clause** In some states, a voting law would have a clause called a **grandfather clause**. They said that a person had the right to vote if his grandfather had the right to vote. Few African American men could qualify because none of their grandfathers, who had been slaves, had the right to vote.

- **Poll tax** A tax that a person must pay to be allowed to vote is called a **poll tax**. Some states charged a poll tax. Since most former slaves were very poor, they could not pay the tax. Therefore, they could not vote.

People fought to get these laws changed. It took a long time. In 1915, the United States Supreme Court said that grandfather clauses in state laws were unconstitutional. Even so, some states used literacy tests and poll taxes to keep African Americans from voting until the 1960s.

In the 1950s, more and more people began to demand that the federal government protect the right of people to vote. People of all races worked together to change unfair state laws. The people gave speeches and marched in the streets. These actions became known as the **civil rights movement**.

As a result of the civil rights movement in 1964, the Twenty-fourth Amendment was added to the Constitution. The **Twenty-fourth Amendment** says that the right to vote in a national election shall not be denied because a person fails to pay a poll tax or any other tax. Two years later, the Supreme Court said this right also applied to state elections.

In 1965, Congress passed a law called the Voting Rights Act. The Voting Rights Act of 1965 further protected the right to vote for all United States citizens. It forced the states to obey the Constitution. It made it clear that the right to vote could not be denied because of a person's color or race.

How did women gain the right to vote?

For most of our history, women did not have the right to vote. Women are the largest group ever denied the right to vote in our nation.

Women began the national fight to gain the right to vote at a convention held in New York in 1848. Women's rights leaders such as Lucretia Mott and Elizabeth Cady Stanton argued that women should have equal rights with men. They said women's rights could be protected only if women had the right to vote. After the Civil War, many women supported the Fifteenth Amendment that gave African American men the right to vote. They tried hard to win their own right to vote at the same time. In those days, it was common to believe that women should not participate in government. This belief hurt women's chances of winning the right to vote.

The struggle for women's right to vote was long and difficult. Women picketed the White House. They marched in parades in cities and towns. Some women went to the polls and insisted on voting. The most famous leader in the struggle for women's rights was Susan B. Anthony. Anthony was arrested and fined $100 for voting illegally in 1872. She refused to pay the fine and the judge did not force her to.

Women continued to fight and win support for their cause. Then, in 1920, the Nineteenth Amendment was added to the Constitution. The **Nineteenth Amendment** gave women the right to vote. More than 130 years after the Framers signed the Constitution, women finally won the right to vote in all elections in the United States.

What did women like Elizabeth Cady Stanton (left) and Susan B. Anthony (right) do to gain support for women's right to vote?

How did Native Americans gain the right to vote?

Native American tribes governed themselves by their own laws, treaties with the United States, and by special laws passed by Congress. Most Native Americans were not recognized as citizens of the United States. They did not have the right to vote.

A law passed in 1924 recognized Native Americans as citizens of the United States. This law gave them the right to vote in both state and federal elections.

How did eighteen-year-olds gain the right to vote?

In 1970, only four states let citizens younger than twenty-one vote. In that year, thousands of young Americans were fighting a war in Vietnam. Many of them were under twenty-one years of age.

People argued that if eighteen-year-olds were old enough to fight, then they were old enough to vote. In March 1971, the Twenty-sixth Amendment was added to the Constitution. The **Twenty-sixth Amendment** gives citizens eighteen years of age or older the right to vote in all elections.

The people who fought for the young adults' right to vote believed they would use this right. Today, however, fewer eighteen- to twenty-four-year-olds vote than any other age group.

How did Native Americans gain the right to vote?

Who is eligible to vote today?

Today, state governments still make decisions about voting rights. All the states have passed laws saying that only citizens can vote. The states limit the right to vote to people who are residents of the state and to those who register to vote. Some states do not allow people who have been found guilty of serious crimes to vote.

The protection of the right of all citizens to vote is now much better than in the past. However, there are still controversies about some state laws that people claim unfairly limit the right to vote of some citizens.

Reviewing and Using the Lesson

1. In the early years of our nation, why did the states only give the right to vote to white men who owned property?

2. Explain how African American men gained the right to vote. What laws had to be changed to make voting rights for African Americans fair?

3. Explain how women gained the right to vote. Why do you think women were not given the right to vote in the first place?

4. Why did Native Americans not have the right to vote? How did this change?

5. Why was the right to vote given to eighteen-year-olds?

Activities

1. With your teacher's help, invite someone from the League of Women Voters to come to your class to discuss elections in your state. Prepare questions to ask your guest before the visit.

2. Learn more about women's struggle for the right to vote. Share what you learned with your class.

3. Make posters encouraging people to vote, especially eighteen- to twenty-four-year-olds.

4. Find out how a citizen can register to vote in your state. Get a copy of a voter registration form. Share what you learned with your class.

5. Write a story with the title "Every Vote Counts." In the story, show how just one person's vote can make a difference. Read your story to the class.

UNIT
5

What are the responsibilities of citizens?

UNIT

5

What are the responsibilities of citizens?

In this text, you have studied the principles and history of the United States Constitution. You learned why and how the Founders organized our government the way they did. You learned that the purpose of government is to protect our rights and to provide for the common good. You also learned that the power of our government comes from the people. The people delegate certain powers to the government.

It is important that our government does its job well. Government cannot do a good job if citizens do not participate. In this unit, you will learn about the United States and its place in world affairs. You will examine the responsibilities of citizens. You also will look at ways in which citizens can take part in government. You will discuss some important issues. For example, how might you balance your self-interest with the common good? What might you do when you think that a law is unfair?

It is very important for us to participate in our government. You should decide for yourself what you ought to do as a citizen of the United States.

KEY TOPICS

- citizenship
- common good
- Declaration of Independence in world affairs
- participation in government
- rights and responsibilities
- self-interest
- U.S. Constitution and Bill of Rights in world affairs

LESSON 22

What is the role of the United States in the world today?

LESSON PURPOSE

Your studies would not be complete if you did not think about the role of the United States in the world today. In this lesson, you will learn some ways that countries interact with one another.

You will also learn how some of the ideas about government in the Declaration of Independence and in the United States Constitution and Bill of Rights have influenced people in other countries.

LESSON OBJECTIVES

When you have finished this lesson, you should be able to

- ❑ explain how other countries have influenced the United States,
- ❑ identify some of the ways countries interact with each other,
- ❑ describe what powers our Constitution gives our government to deal with other countries, and
- ❑ explain how the Declaration of Independence, Constitution, and Bill of Rights have influenced other countries.

TERMS TO KNOW

- diplomacy
- humanitarian
- United Nations

How have other countries influenced the United States?

Many of the ideals of government that you have studied came from other countries. A country consists of territory, people, government, and laws. The Founders learned about government from studying the histories of the countries of ancient Greece and Rome. From the Greeks and Romans, they learned about republican government, civic virtue, and the common good.

The European philosophers also had a great impact on the Founders. The theories of Baron de Montesquieu from France influenced their thinking about separation of powers. The writings of John Locke from Great Britain guided their thinking about natural rights.

The Founders had also enjoyed the rights of Englishmen. Among these were the right to trial by jury, the right to be secure in one's home, and the right to express one's views about taxes through one's representative in government.

How do countries of the world interact?

Today, events in the United States influence many countries around the globe. What happens in other countries also affects the United States. It is important that we know how countries interact with one another and that we are informed about world events.

Here are some ways in which countries interact with one another.

How might scientific exchanges aid both the United States and other countries?

Why do countries trade goods and services?

- **Culture, science, and business exchanges** People travel all over the world. People living in different countries share ideas. Doctors, scientists, and business people from many countries meet to share advances in their fields. Students and teachers live with families in other countries to learn about their cultures. Artists show their work in the museums of other countries.

- **Humanitarian aid** The term **humanitarian** means to show concern for the pain and suffering of others. During natural disasters, such as floods and earthquakes, countries help the victims in other countries by giving humanitarian aid. Countries send medicine, food, and shelter to suffering people.

- **Trade** Countries buy from and sell factory and farm goods to one another in world markets.

- **Diplomacy** The term **diplomacy** means to carry on a formal relationship with the governments of other countries. The official representatives of countries meet and discuss things important to both countries. They work to find ways to solve common problems in a peaceful manner.

- **Treaties and agreements** Countries make treaties and agreements. They agree to promote trade among themselves. They agree to do certain things to protect the environment. Some agree to help each other in time of war.

Why was the United Nations created? What power does the organization have?

- **Military force** When two or more countries cannot resolve their disagreements peacefully, they sometimes use military force. The disagreement might result in a war.

There is no single organization in the world that has the power to force countries to settle conflicts peacefully. There are some organizations that help countries reach agreements without going to war. One such organization is the **United Nations**.

The United Nations was created in 1945. It was meant to be a general international organization to maintain peace and security for its members. The delegates of fifty nations drew up the United Nations Charter, which was adopted unanimously.

What powers does the U.S. Constitution give to the government to deal with other countries?

Each branch of government has certain powers. These powers come from the Constitution. The Constitution gives each branch the following powers to deal with other countries.

- **Congress** The U.S. Congress has the power to regulate commerce with other countries and with Native American tribes. It can declare war, approve treaties, approve ambassadors, raise and support armies, and punish piracies and crimes committed on the high seas.

- **President** The president has the power to lead military forces as commander in chief, grant pardons, make treaties, and name ambassadors with the approval of Congress.

- **U.S. Supreme Court** The Supreme Court has the power to hear all cases affecting ambassadors, cases in which the United States is a party, and cases involving a foreign state, its citizens or subjects.

How have the Declaration of Independence and the United States Constitution and Bill of Rights influenced other countries?

The United States has made many contributions to the world. Some of these include advanced medical and industrial technology and the personal computer. All the discoveries and inventions that we as a nation have contributed to the world are important. But they are not as valuable or long-lasting as the democratic ideas expressed in the Declaration of Independence and the United States Constitution and Bill of Rights. Some of these ideas are listed here.

1. Power comes from the people, and the people are the ultimate source of the authority of their government.

2. People in government are the servants of the people. They are not the masters of the people.

3. All people are political equals. No person's vote should count more than another's.

4. The people delegate their powers to their government. They consent to be governed only so long as those in power fulfill their responsibilities. They can take back those powers and change their government.

5. The purposes of government are to protect the people's rights to life, liberty, and property, and to promote the common good.

6. A nation's constitution should be approved by the people and serve as a higher law that everyone must obey, including the people and those serving in their government.

7. A nation's constitution should include a list of the rights of the people.

During the nineteenth and twentieth centuries, the American ideal of self-government spread around the world. People from many countries read and studied the ideas in the Declaration of Independence and the Constitution and Bill of Rights. These documents influenced other countries to adopt similar ideas about government.

The American Revolution gave hope to many people in Europe and Latin America who wanted to promote democratic change in their own countries. The French Constitution of 1791 included many ideas from the United States. The Declaration of Independence and the U.S. Constitution and Bill of Rights also inspired Latin American leaders. Among these leaders were José de San Martín in Argentina, Simón Bolívar in Venezuela, and Miguel Hidalgo in Mexico.

Throughout our history, we have thought of citizenship only in terms of our country. The issues that citizens deal with today are becoming increasingly international.

How have America's founding documents influenced other countries?

What countries have experienced democratic change in the last two hundred years?

What Do You Think?

How do countries influence each other?

Work with a partner. Discuss the following questions. Be prepared to share your ideas with the class.

1. What events in the United States today might have an effect on other people of the world?
2. What events in the world today might have an effect on citizens of the United States?
3. What do citizens of the United States gain from our relationships with other countries of the world? What do citizens in other countries gain?
4. Why is it important that countries be able to have a free exchange of ideas?

Reviewing and Using the Lesson

1. List some things that countries do to carry out their relationships with other countries.

2. What powers does the U.S. Constitution give the national government to deal with other countries?

3. List some of the ideas in the Declaration of Independence and in the Constitution and Bill of Rights that have influenced government in other countries.

Activities

1. Learn more about the United Nations. Why and how was the United Nations established? What does the United Nations do? Share what you learned with your class.

2. Suppose you make a telephone call to a friend or relative in South Africa or in Jordan. Suppose you send a letter to China using a stamp from the United States. Learn about international agreements that make it possible for your telephone call or letter to reach its destination. Find information about the Universal Postal Union or the International Telecommunication Union.

3. Select one of the following leaders of the Latin American revolutions of the 1800s. Learn about the person's life. Learn about how the ideas in the Declaration of Independence and the U.S. Constitution and Bill of Rights influenced his thinking about government.
   - José de San Martín
   - Miguel Hidalgo
   - Simón Bolívar
   - Bernardo O'Higgins

4. Choose one of the following countries: China, Colombia, France, Israel, Panama, Russia, Saudi Arabia, or Vietnam. Learn about the country's relationship with the United States in the past and today. Share what you learned with the class.

LESSON 23

What are some important responsibilities of citizens?

LESSON PURPOSE

Suppose your government does everything it can to protect your rights. Is this enough? Will your rights be protected? Do we have any responsibility to protect not only our own rights, but each other's as well? In this lesson, you will discuss some important questions about the responsibilities of citizens. You must develop your own answers to these questions. We hope this lesson helps you develop good answers.

LESSON OBJECTIVES

When you have finished this lesson, you should be able to

- ❑ explain some of the responsibilities related to important rights,
- ❑ evaluate a situation in which the rights of individuals conflict with the common good, and
- ❑ take and defend a position on the issue.

TERMS TO KNOW

- citizen
- naturalized citizens
- resident aliens

How does a person become a naturalized citizen?

Who is a citizen of the United States?

A **citizen** is a member of an official political body, such as a nation or a state. Citizens of the United States are those who are

- born in the United States;
- born to United States citizens living in another country;
- born elsewhere, living legally in the United States, and have passed a test on the Constitution and history of the United States to become **naturalized citizens**;
- children of naturalized citizens who were under the age of eighteen when their parents became citizens.

The national government protects the rights of all people who live in the United States. People who are not citizens, but who live legally in the United States, are called **resident aliens**. Resident aliens enjoy most of the rights of citizens. They have the same right to due process of law as citizens.

Resident aliens do not have the right to vote, serve on a jury, or run for public office. Like citizens, resident aliens have a responsibility to obey the law.

Is a good constitution enough to protect your rights?

The Framers planned our government carefully. They organized it so its powers were limited. They separated the powers of our government among three different branches. They balanced the powers among these branches. They provided ways each branch could check or limit the powers of the other branches. Finally, they added a Bill of Rights. The Bill of Rights now protects our rights from unfair treatment by our national, state, and local governments.

Some of the Framers believed they had organized the government very well. They believed the way they planned the government was enough to make sure our rights and the common good would be protected.

Other Framers did not agree. They believed that the government would only work well if there were good people running it. They also believed it would only succeed if the citizens were good citizens.

Today, most people agree that a well-written constitution is not enough to protect our rights. We need to elect leaders who will make and enforce laws that protect our rights and promote our welfare.

Even a good constitution and good leaders may not be enough. If we want to protect our rights and welfare, we, the people, have certain responsibilities to fulfill. Let's examine what some of these responsibilities might be.

What should you do to preserve your rights to life, liberty, and the pursuit of happiness?

Critical Thinking Exercise

What responsibilities go along with these rights?

Let's examine some responsibilities that might go along with your basic rights. Work in small groups. Each group should answer the questions about one of the rights listed below. Then each group should share its ideas with the class.

Group 1: The right to freedom of expression

Suppose you attend a meeting of students in your school. The purpose of the meeting is to suggest rules for the playground. Every student has the right to speak and to make suggestions.

1. What should be your responsibilities for the way you speak and what you say?
2. What should be your responsibilities toward the right of others to speak?
3. What responsibilities should the other students have to you and your right to speak?
4. Government may not unfairly limit your right to express your ideas freely. What responsibilities should you have that might go along with this right?
5. Suppose no one fulfilled the responsibilities that you have discussed. What might happen to our right to freedom of expression?

What responsibilities do you have toward other people who want to share their opinions?

What does it mean to practice religion responsibly?

Group 2: The right to freedom of religion

Suppose you believe in a particular religion. You attend a church, meeting hall, mosque, or temple in your community.

1. What responsibilities should you have in the way you practice your religious beliefs?
2. What responsibilities should you have toward the right of other people to practice their religious beliefs?
3. What responsibilities should people who hold different religious beliefs have toward your right to practice your religious beliefs?
4. Government may not interfere with your right to believe as you wish. It may not unfairly limit your right to practice your religious beliefs. What responsibilities should you have that go along with these rights?
5. Suppose no one fulfilled the responsibilities that you have discussed. What might happen to our right to freedom of religion?

Group 3: The right to the equal protection of the laws

Suppose your city government officials are planning a picnic for the people who live in your community.

1. What responsibilities should officials have to you regardless of your age, gender, race, or religion?

2. If you volunteer to help plan the city's picnic, what responsibilities should you have to others?

3. Government is not permitted to favor some people over others because of their age, gender, race, or religion. What responsibilities should you have that go along with this right?

4. Suppose no one fulfilled the responsibilities that you have discussed. What might happen to our right to the equal protection of the laws?

What ideas should people consider when deciding how to vote in a school election?

Group 4: The right to due process of law

Suppose someone accused you of doing something wrong in your school.

1. What responsibilities should the accuser have toward you?
2. If you were the one who accused another student of doing something wrong, what responsibilities should you have toward her or him?
3. Government must be fair to you when it is gathering information and making decisions. What responsibilities should you have that go along with this right?
4. Suppose no one fulfilled the responsibilities that you have discussed. What might happen to our right to due process of the law?

Group 5: The right to vote and run for public office

Suppose you are about to vote in a school election. You must choose between two people running for class president.

1. What responsibilities should you have?
2. You have decided to vote for Bill. Your friends want to vote for John. What responsibilities should you have about their right to vote?
3. What responsibilities should they have about your right to vote?
4. When you are eighteen, you will have the right to vote in government elections. You will also have the right to run for some public offices. What responsibilities should go along with these rights?
5. Suppose that no one fulfilled the responsibilities that you have discussed. What might happen to our right to vote?

Reviewing and Using the Lesson

1. How does a person become a citizen of the United States?
2. What are some responsibilities of citizens? Why is fulfilling these responsibilities important?
3. What are some responsibilities that go along with your right to free expression, freedom of religion, equal protection of the laws, due process of law, and the right to vote?

Activities

1. Find more information about how a person can become a naturalized citizen of the United States.
2. Do some research on a famous naturalized citizen. What contributions has that person made to the United States?
3. Create a poster that shows some rights of citizens and the responsibilities that those rights carry.
4. Write a story about what can happen in a community where people do not exercise their responsibility to be good citizens.
5. Interview someone who is a resident alien. In a report to the class, explain the person's opinion about whether he or she wants to be a citizen of the United States.

LESSON 24

How can citizens promote the common good?

LESSON PURPOSE

In this lesson, you will examine some responsibilities that we all have to promote the common good. We will also look at ways we can participate in making decisions about protecting our rights and the common good.

LESSON OBJECTIVES

When you have finished this lesson, you should be able to

- ❑ explain the importance of promoting the common good,
- ❑ explain why it is sometimes difficult to agree upon what is the common good, and
- ❑ explain why education is important in preparing citizens to participate in their government and the reasons why they should participate.

How can people your age contribute to the common good?

How do we decide what is best for everyone?

When you studied the ideas of natural rights, you learned that the purpose of government is to protect our rights to life, liberty, and property. When we choose a government that promises to protect these rights, we protect our self-interest. We want to make sure that government fulfills its duties to us as individuals.

When you studied the ideas of republican government, you learned that the government and its citizens have a duty to serve the common good. Each citizen works cooperatively with the government and each other for the good of the whole community. In some situations, this might mean that we should put aside our own self-interest for the common good.

In some situations, the common good is quite clear. For example, it is good for all of us to live in a healthy environment. Our country needs to be protected by our armed forces. In other situations, citizens might disagree about the common good. For example, people disagree about whether it is good for everyone to begin each school day with a prayer.

Some people might also disagree about how to serve the common good. We know that protecting the environment serves the common good. But, some ways of protecting the environment might endanger people's jobs and violate property rights. Sometimes it is difficult to decide between our self-interest and the common good.

Critical Thinking Exercise

How Should the Town Council Vote?

Suppose the town council calls for a public hearing to seek opinions and advice from the people living and working in Smallville, USA. The council has arranged a public hearing on Monday at seven o'clock. They have invited the people who live and work in the town to attend the hearing. They are hoping for a good turnout. The town council wants to get some good ideas that might help to solve the town's problem.

Getting Ready for the Public Hearing

Read the facts about the problem in Smallville. Prepare to play the role of one of the groups described after the story. Each group should prepare a presentation to make at the public hearing. The town council will ask your opinion about solving the problem.

Problems in Smallville, USA

Imagine that you live in a small community. Most of the people in Smallville work in one large factory. The smoke from the factory pollutes the air and is a danger to everyone's health. The smoke also pollutes the air of communities nearby.

It would be very expensive to stop the pollution. The owners of the factory say they cannot afford to buy the machinery needed to stop pollution. They would lose money and might not be able to stay in business. If the factory closed, the owners say that many people would lose their jobs. There are no other good jobs available nearby, and many people would be without a job.

The town council is looking for ways to solve the problem and is hoping that the public hearing will help them to make a decision on how to solve the town's problem with pollution. The town council is supposed to protect the people's rights. It is also supposed to support the common good.

Group 1: The Town Council Members

The town council must find a way to rid the town of air pollution that is harming the health of the people living in town and in communities nearby. The council does not want the factory to close and cause most of the town residents to lose their jobs. The council wants to speak with groups that have valuable information about the situation. The town council must consider the following:

1. What might be some self-interests of the people who live in the community?

Critical Thinking Exercise

2. Are there individual rights that should be considered?

3. What might be the common good of the community?

4. To make a good and fair decision, what issues does the town council have to consider?

5. What are the advantages and disadvantages of each solution suggested?

After the hearing, the town council will make a decision.

Group 2: Owners of the Factory
You earn a living from the factory, and you employ many workers who also earn their living from the factory. If the town council requires you to install expensive machinery onto the smokestacks of your factory, you would not be able to afford the cost and have to close the factory.

What are some rights and responsibilities of citizens in a free society?

Group 3: Employees of the Factory

You have worked in the factory for many years. Your father and your grandfather worked in this factory. You do not want to lose your job because you realize there are no other good jobs in Smallville.

Group 4: Citizens for Better Health

You think that pollution is a direct cause of serious health problems in your town. You want machinery installed to limit the amount of smoke the factory can produce.

Group 5: Citizens for a Pollution-free Environment

You believe that pollution is damaging animal habitats and harming trees and other plants in nearby wooded areas. You believe that environmental agencies should be contacted to give advice.

Taking Part in the Public Hearing

1. The president of the town council will start the meeting.
2. Each group has four minutes to explain its position to the council.
3. After each presentation, the council member may ask questions of the group for two minutes. Each person in the group should help answer the questions.
4. After hearing all the groups, the town council will meet and decide what to do.

Talking It Over

1. Do you agree with the town council's decision?
2. Why might citizens disagree about which opinion is most important for the town?
3. Are there any ways to solve the problem other than those discussed in the hearing?
4. Did you change your opinion after listening to all of the groups? If you did, which argument convinced you?

What are some ways that you can participate in our government?

How can you participate in your government?

Our government is a government of the people, by the people, and for the people. You are a part of the people. We, the people, run our government. We elect people to work for us in our government.

We need to be sure they do a good job. If they do, we will vote for them again. If they do not, we may want to vote for others to take their place. We participate in government to protect our rights and to promote the common good.

You cannot vote until you are eighteen. However, you can still participate in our government. One of the most important things you can do is something you have already started to do. You can learn something about our government. You can learn what it is supposed to do. You can learn how it works. You can learn what rights you have. Finally, you can think about what responsibilities you should carry out.

Thomas Jefferson and other important Founders thought that all people should have an opportunity to get an education. They thought the main purpose of education should be to prepare you to become a thoughtful and responsible citizen. They knew our government could only work well if the people are well educated. Jefferson said, "If a nation expects to be ignorant and free, … it expects what never was and what never will be."

You can also participate by keeping informed about what your government is doing. You can keep informed by reading newspapers, magazines, and responsible websites. You can listen to the news on the radio and watch it on television. You can discuss the actions of government with your parents and friends. You can protect your rights and the rights of others. If there is a law or problem you feel strongly about, you can express your opinion. You can tell your friends, and you can write to members of your government.

You can participate by volunteering to help people in your community. You can participate by taking part in the government of your classroom and your school. You can start now to be an informed and effective citizen.

What responsibilities will you fulfill?

You have learned a great deal about our nation's government. You have learned about the government's responsibilities and your rights. You have also discussed some of the responsibilities of citizens.

You have inherited a free society. It is your society. You are free to make many choices. You are free to choose what kind of citizen you want to be. You can help keep your society free. You can help make sure all people's rights are protected. You can help promote our common good. We hope that this book helps you make wise decisions about what kind of citizen you want to be.

What are some rights and responsibilities of citizens in a free society?

Reviewing and Using the Lesson

1. How can schools help students become good citizens?
2. What are some ways you can participate in your government now?
3. Does a good citizen have a responsibility to try to improve the lives of people who need help? Why or why not?
4. What responsibilities should a citizen take to protect or promote the welfare of people in other countries? Explain your position.
5. Why is it necessary that a citizen balance his or her self-interest with the common good?

Activities

1. Make a list of things you can do for your community. Put these things in two columns. At the top of one column write Political Actions, and at the top of the other write Social Actions. Explain to your class the difference between these two kinds of community responsibilities.
2. Go to your library or use the internet to research the life of someone from your city, state, or tribal reservation who put the common good before his or her own self-interest. Write a short report to present to your class.
3. Make a poster that shows how students in your grade, but in another state or country, are engaged in good citizenship.

Reference

THE DECLARATION OF INDEPENDENCE

July 4, 1776

The Declaration of Independence was passed by Congress on July 2, 1776, and issued on July 4, announcing the separation of the "United Colonies" from Britain and the formation of a new nation, the United States of America. The document lists reasons for the separation and a philosophical argument in defense of action.

In CONGRESS, July 4, 1776.

The unanimous Declaration of the thirteen united States of America,

WHEN in the Course of human Events, it becomes necessary for one People to dissolve the Political Bands which have connected them with another, and to assume among the Powers of the Earth, the separate and equal Station to which the Laws of Nature and of Nature's God entitle them, a decent Respect to the Opinions of Mankind requires that they should declare the causes which impel them to the Separation.

We hold these Truths to be self-evident, that all Men are created equal, that they are endowed by their Creator with certain unalienable Rights, that among these are Life, Liberty, and the Pursuit of Happiness—That to secure these Rights, Governments are instituted among Men, deriving their just Powers from the Consent of the Governed, that whenever any Form of Government becomes destructive of these Ends it is the Right of the People to alter or to abolish it, and to institute new Government, laying its Foundation on such Principles, and organizing its Powers in such Form, as to them shall seem most likely to effect their Safety and Happiness. Prudence, indeed, will dictate that Governments long established should not be changed for light and transient Causes; and accordingly all Experience hath shewn, that Mankind are more disposed to suffer, while Evils are sufferable, than to right themselves by abolishing the Forms to which they are accustomed. But when a long Train of Abuses and Usurpations, pursuing invariably the same Object, evinces a Design to reduce them under absolute Despotism, it is their Right, it is their Duty, to throw off such Government, and to provide new Guards for their future Security. Such has been the patient Sufferance of these Colonies; and such is now the Necessity which constrains them to alter their former Systems of Government. The History of the present King of Great-Britain is a History of repeated Injuries and Usurpations, all having in direct Object the Establishment of an absolute Tyranny over these States. To prove this, let Facts be submitted to a candid World.

He has refused his Assent to Laws, the most wholesome and necessary for the public Good.

He has forbidden his Governors to pass Laws of immediate and pressing Importance, unless suspended in their Operation till his Assent should be obtained; and when so suspended, he has utterly neglected to attend to them.

He has refused to pass other Laws for the Accommodation of large Districts of People, unless those People would relinquish the Right of Representation in the Legislature, a Right inestimable to them, and formidable to Tyrants only.

He has called together Legislative Bodies at Places unusual, uncomfortable, and distant from the Depository of their public Records, for the sole Purpose of fatiguing them into Compliance with his Measures.

He has dissolved Representative Houses repeatedly, for opposing with manly Firmness his Invasions on the Rights of the People.

He has refused for a long Time, after such Dissolutions, to cause others to be elected; whereby the Legislative Powers, incapable of Annihilation, have returned to the People at large for their exercise; the State remaining in the mean time exposed to all the Dangers of Invasions from without, and Convulsions within.

He has endeavored to prevent the Population of these States; for that Purpose obstructing the Laws for Naturalization of Foreigners; refusing to pass others to encourage their Migrations hither, and raising the Conditions of new Appropriations of Lands.

He has obstructed the Administration of Justice, by refusing his Assent to Laws for establishing Judiciary Powers.

He has made Judges dependent on his Will alone, for the Tenure of their Offices, and the Amount and Payment of their Salaries.

He has erected a Multitude of new Offices, and sent hither Swarms of Officers to harass our People and eat out their Substance.

He has kept among us, in Times of Peace, Standing Armies, without the consent of our Legislatures.

He has affected to render the Military independent of and superior to the Civil Power.

He has combined with others to subject us to a Jurisdiction foreign to our Constitution, and unacknowledged by our Laws; giving his Assent to their Acts of pretended Legislation:

For quartering large Bodies of Armed Troops among us:

For protecting them, by a mock Trial, from Punishment for any Murders which they should commit on the Inhabitants of these States:

For cutting off our Trade with all Parts of the World:

For imposing Taxes on us without our Consent:

For depriving us, in many Cases, of the Benefits of Trial by Jury:

For transporting us beyond Seas to be tried for pretended Offenses:

For abolishing the free System of English Laws in a neighbouring Province, establishing therein an Arbitrary Government, and enlarging its Boundaries, so as to render it at once an Example and fit Instrument for introducing the same absolute Rule into these Colonies:

For taking away our Charters, abolishing our most valuable Laws, and altering fundamentally the Forms of our Governments:

For suspending our own Legislatures, and declaring themselves invested with Power to legislate for us in all Cases whatsoever.

He has abdicated Government here, by declaring us out of his Protection and waging War against us.

He has plundered our Seas, ravaged our Coasts, burnt our Towns, and destroyed the Lives of our People.

He is, at this Time, transporting large Armies of foreign Mercenaries to compleat the Works of Death, Desolation, and Tyranny, already begun with circumstances of Cruelty and Perfidy, scarcely paralleled in the most barbarous Ages, and totally unworthy the Head of a civilized Nation.

He has constrained our fellow Citizens taken Captive on the high Seas to bear Arms against their Country, to become the Executioners of their Friends and Brethren, or to fall themselves by their Hands.

He has excited domestic Insurrections amongst us, and has endeavoured to bring on the Inhabitants of our Frontiers, the merciless Indian Savages, whose known Rule of Warfare, is an undistinguished Destruction, of all Ages, Sexes and Conditions.

In every stage of these Oppressions we have Petitioned for Redress in the most humble Terms: Our repeated Petitions have been answered only by repeated Injury. A Prince, whose Character is thus marked by every act which may define a Tyrant, is unfit to be the Ruler of a free People.

Nor have we been wanting in Attentions to our British Brethren. We have warned them from Time to Time of Attempts by their Legislature to extend an unwarrantable Jurisdiction over us. We have reminded them of the Circumstances of our Emigration and Settlement here. We have appealed to their native Justice and Magnanimity, and we have conjured them by the Ties of our common Kindred to disavow these Usurpations, which, would inevitably interrupt our Connections and Correspondence. They too have been deaf to the Voice of Justice and of Consanguinity. We must, therefore, acquiesce in the Necessity, which denounces our Separation, and hold them, as we hold the rest of Mankind, Enemies in War, in Peace, Friends.

We, therefore, the Representatives of the UNITED STATES OF AMERICA, in GENERAL CONGRESS, Assembled, appealing to the Supreme Judge of the World for the Rectitude of our Intentions, do, in the Name, and by Authority of the good People of these Colonies, solemnly Publish and Declare, That these United Colonies are, and of Right ought to be, FREE AND INDEPENDENT STATES; that they are absolved from all Allegiance to the British Crown, and that all political Connection between them and the State of Great Britain, is and ought to be totally dissolved; and that as FREE AND INDEPENDENT STATES, they have full Power to levy War, conclude Peace, contract Alliances, establish Commerce, and to do all other Acts and Things which INDEPENDENT STATES may of right do. And for the support of this Declaration, with a firm Reliance on the Protection of divine Providence, we mutually pledge to each other our Lives, our Fortunes, and our sacred Honor.

Signed by ORDER and in BEHALF of the CONGRESS,
JOHN HANCOCK, PRESIDENT.

New-Hampshire

Josiah Bartlett,

Wm. Whipple,

Matthew Thornton.

Massachusetts-Bay

Saml. Adams,

John Adams,

Robt. Treat Paine,

Elbridge Gerry.

Rhode-Island and Providence, &c.

Step. Hopkins,

William Ellery.

Connecticut

Roger Sherman,

Saml. Huntington,

Wm. Williams,

Oliver Wolcott.

New-York

Wm. Floyd,

Phil. Livingston,

Frans. Lewis,

Lewis Morris.

New-Jersey

Richd. Stockton,

Jno. Witherspoon,

Fras. Hopkinson,

John Hart,

Abra. Clark.

Pennsylvania

Robt. Morris,

Benjamin Rush,

Benja. Franklin,

John Morton,

Geo. Clymer,

Jas. Smith,

Geo. Taylor,

James Wilson,

Geo. Ross.

Delaware

Casar Rodney,

Geo. Read,

(Tho M:Kean.)

Maryland

Samuel Chase,

Wm. Paca,

Thos. Stone,

Charles Carroll, of Carrollton.

Virginia

George Wythe,

Richard Henry Lee,

Ths. Jefferson,

Benja. Harrison,

Thos. Nelson, jr.,

Francis Lightfoot Lee,

Carter Braxton.

North-Carolina

Wm. Hooper,

Joseph Hewes,

John Penn.

South-Carolina

Edward Rutledge,

Thos. Heyward, junr.,

Thomas Lynch, junr.,

Arthur Middleton.

Georgia

Button Gwinnett,

Lyman Hall,

Geo. Walton.

THE CONSTITUTION OF THE UNITED STATES OF AMERICA
SEPTEMBER 17, 1787

The Constitution was adopted in Philadelphia on September 17, 1787, by the Constitutional Convention and was declared ratified on July 2, 1788.

PREAMBLE

We the People of the United States, in Order to form a more perfect Union, establish Justice, insure domestic tranquility, provide for the common defense, promote the general Welfare, and secure the Blessings of Liberty to ourselves and our Posterity, do ordain and establish this Constitution for the United States of America.

ARTICLE I

THE LEGISLATIVE BRANCH

Section 1

All legislative Powers herein granted shall be vested in a Congress of the United States, which shall consist of a Senate and House of Representatives.

Section 2

House of Representatives: Organization and Power of Impeachment

1 The House of Representatives shall be composed of Members chosen every second Year by the People of the several States, and the Electors in each State shall have the Qualifications requisite for Electors of the most numerous Branch of the State Legislature.

2 No Person shall be a Representative who shall not have attained to the Age of twenty five Years, and been seven Years a Citizen of the United States, and who shall not, when elected, be an Inhabitant of that State in which he shall be chosen.

3 [Representatives and direct Taxes shall be apportioned among the several States which may be included within this Union, according to their respective Numbers, which shall be determined by adding to the whole Number of free Persons, including those bound to Service for a Term of Years, and excluding Indians not taxed, three fifths of all other Persons.]* The actual Enumeration shall be made within three Years after the first Meeting of the Congress of the United States, and within every subsequent Term of ten Years, in such Manner as they shall by Law direct. The number of Representatives shall not exceed one for every thirty Thousand, but each State shall have at Least one Representative; and until such enumeration shall be made, the State of New Hampshire shall be entitled to choose three, Massachusetts eight, Rhode Island and Providence Plantations one, Connecticut five, New York six, New Jersey four, Pennsylvania eight, Delaware one, Maryland six, Virginia ten, North Carolina five, South Carolina five, and Georgia three.

4 When vacancies happen in the Representation from any State, the Executive Authority thereof shall issue Writs of Election to fill such Vacancies.

5 The House of Representatives shall choose their Speaker and other Officers; and shall have the sole Power of Impeachment.

Section 3

The Senate: Organization and Powers to Try Cases of Impeachment

1 The Senate of the United States shall be composed of two Senators from each State, chosen [by the Legislature thereof,]** for six Years; and each Senator shall have one Vote.

2 Immediately after they shall be assembled in Consequence of the first Election, they shall be divided as equally as may be into three Classes. The seats of the Senators of the first Class shall be vacated at the Expiration of the second Year, of the second Class at the Expiration of the fourth

* *Changed by Section 2 of the Fourteenth Amendment*

** *Changed by the Seventeenth Amendment*

Year, and of the third Class at the Expiration of the sixth Year, so that one third may be chosen every second Year; [and if Vacancies happen by Resignation, or otherwise, during the Recess of the Legislature of any State, the Executive thereof may make temporary Appointments until the next Meeting of the Legislature, which shall then fill such Vacancies.]*

3 No Person shall be a Senator who shall not have attained to the Age of thirty Years, and been nine Years a Citizen of the United States, and who shall not, when elected, be an Inhabitant of that State for which he shall be chosen.

4 The Vice President of the United States shall be President of the Senate, but shall have no Vote, unless they be equally divided.

5 The Senate shall choose their other officers, and also a President pro tempore, in the Absence of the Vice President, or when he shall exercise the Office of President of the United States.

6 The Senate shall have the sole Power to try all Impeachments. When sitting for that Purpose, they shall be on Oath or Affirmation. When the President of the United States is tried, the Chief Justice shall preside; And no person shall be convicted without the Concurrence of two thirds of the Members present.

7 Judgment in Cases of Impeachment shall not extend further than to removal from Office, and disqualification to hold and enjoy any Office of honor, Trust or Profit under the United States; but the Party convicted shall nevertheless be liable and subject to Indictment, Trial, Judgment and Punishment, according to Law.

Section 4

Elections and Meeting of Congress

1 The Times, Places and Manner of holding Elections for Senators and Representatives shall be prescribed in each State by the Legislature thereof; but the Congress may at any time by Law make or alter such Regulations, except as to the Places of choosing Senators.

2 The Congress shall assemble at least once in every Year, and such Meeting shall be [on the first Monday in December,]** unless they shall by Law appoint a different Day.

* *Changed by Section 2 of the Fourteenth Amendment*
** *Changed by the Seventeenth Amendment*

Section 5

Congress's Rules of Procedure, Powers, Quorum, Journals, Meetings, Adjournments

1 Each House shall be the Judge of the Elections, Returns and Qualifications of its own Members, and a Majority of each shall constitute a Quorum to do Business; but a smaller Number may adjourn from day to day, and may be authorized to compel the Attendance of absent Members, in such Manner, and under such Penalties as each House may provide.

2 Each House may determine the Rules of its Proceedings, punish its members for disorderly Behavior, and, with the Concurrence of two thirds, expel a Member.

3 Each House shall keep a Journal of its Proceedings, and from time to time publish the same, excepting such Parts as may in their Judgment require Secrecy; and the Yeas and Nays of the Members of either House on any question shall, at the Desire of one fifth of those Present, be entered on the Journal.

4 Neither House, during the Session of Congress, shall, without the Consent of the other, adjourn for more than three days, nor to any other Place than that in which the two Houses shall be sitting.

Section 6

Pay, Privileges, Limitations

1 The Senators and Representatives shall receive a Compensation for their Services, to be ascertained by Law, and paid out of the Treasury of the United States. They shall in all cases, except Treason, Felony and Breach of the Peace, be privileged from Arrest during their Attendance at the Session of their respective Houses, and in going to and returning from the same; and for any Speech or Debate in either House, they shall not be questioned in any other Place.

2 No Senator or Representative shall, during the Time for which he was elected, be appointed to any civil Office under the Authority of the United States, which shall have been created, or the Emoluments whereof shall have been increased during such time; and no Person holding any Office under the United States, shall be a Member of either House during his Continuance in Office.

Section 7

Procedure in Passing Bills, President's Veto Power

1 All Bills for raising Revenue shall originate in the House of Representatives; but the Senate may propose or concur with Amendments as on other Bills.

2 Every Bill which shall have passed the House of Representatives and the Senate, shall, before it becomes a Law, be presented to the President of the United States; if he approves he shall sign it, but if not he shall return it, with his Objections, to that House in which it shall have originated, who shall enter the Objections at large on their Journal, and proceed to reconsider it. If after such Reconsideration two thirds of that House shall agree to pass the Bill, it shall be sent, together with the Objections, to the other House, by which it shall likewise be reconsidered, and if approved by two thirds of that House, it shall become a Law. But in all such Cases the Votes of both Houses shall be determined by Yeas and Nays, and the Names of the Persons voting for and against the Bill shall be entered on the Journal of each House respectively. If any Bill shall not be returned by the President within ten Days (Sundays excepted) after it shall have been presented to him, the Same shall be a Law, in like Manner as if he had signed it, unless the Congress by their adjournment prevent its Return, in which Case it shall not be a Law.

3 Every Order, Resolution, or Vote to which the Concurrence of the Senate and House of Representatives may be necessary (except on a question of Adjournment) shall be presented to the President of the United States; and before the Same shall take Effect, shall be approved by him, or being disapproved by him, shall be repassed by two thirds of the Senate and House of Representatives, according to the Rules and Limitations prescribed in the Case of a Bill.

Section 8

Powers Delegated to Congress

The Congress shall have Power

1 To lay and collect Taxes, Duties, Imposts and Excises, to pay the Debts and provide for the common Defense and general Welfare of the United States; but all Duties, Imposts and Excises shall be uniform throughout the United States;

2 To borrow Money on the credit of the United States;

3 To regulate Commerce with foreign Nations, and among the several States, and with the Indian Tribes;

4 To establish a uniform Rule of Naturalization, and uniform Laws on the subject of Bankruptcies throughout the United States;

5 To coin Money, regulate the Value thereof, and of foreign Coin, and fix the Standard of Weights and Measures;

6 To provide for the Punishment of counterfeiting the Securities and current Coin of the United States;

7 To establish Post Offices and post Roads;

8 To promote the Progress of Science and useful Arts, by securing for limited Times to Authors and Inventors the exclusive Right to their respective Writings and Discoveries;

9 To constitute Tribunals inferior to the Supreme Court;

10 To define and punish Piracies and Felonies committed on the high Seas, and Offenses against the Law of Nations;

11 To declare War, grant Letters of Marque and Reprisal, and make Rules concerning Captures on Land and Water;

12 To raise and support Armies, but no Appropriation of Money to that Use shall be for a longer Term than two Years;

13 To provide and maintain a Navy;

14 To make Rules for the Government and Regulation of the land and naval Forces;

15 To provide for calling forth the Militia to execute the Laws of the Union, suppress Insurrections and repel Invasions;

16 To provide for organizing, arming, and disciplining the Militia, and for governing such Part of them as may be employed in the Service of the United States, reserving to the States respectively, the Appointment of the Officers, and the Authority of training the Militia according to the discipline prescribed by Congress;

17 To exercise exclusive Legislation in all Cases whatsoever, over such District (not exceeding ten Miles square) as may, by Session of particular States, and the Acceptance of Congress, become the Seat of the Government of the United States, and to exercise like Authority over all Places purchased by the Consent of the Legislature of the State in which the Same shall be, for the Erection of Forts, Magazines, Arsenals, dock-Yards and other needful Buildings;—and

18 To make all Laws which shall be necessary and proper for carrying into Execution the foregoing Powers, and all other Powers vested by this Constitution in the Government of the United States, or in any Department or Officer thereof.

Section 9

Powers Denied to Congress

1 The Migration or Importation of such Persons as any of the States now existing shall think proper to admit, shall not be prohibited by the Congress prior to the Year one thousand eight hundred and eight, but a Tax or duty may be imposed on such Importation, not exceeding ten dollars for each Person.

2 The Privilege of the Writ of Habeas Corpus shall not be suspended, unless when in Cases of Rebellion or Invasion the public Safety may require it.

3 No Bill of Attainder or ex post facto Law shall be passed.

4 [No Capitation, or other direct, Tax shall be laid, unless in Proportion to the Census or Enumeration herein before directed to be taken.]*

5 No Tax or Duty shall be laid on Articles exported from any State.

6 No Preference shall be given by any Regulation of Commerce or Revenue to the Ports of one State over those of another; nor shall Vessels bound to, or from, one State, be obliged to enter, clear, or pay Duties in another.

7 No Money shall be drawn from the Treasury, but in Consequence of Appropriations made by Law; and a regular Statement and Account of the Receipts and Expenditures of all public Money shall be published from time to time.

8 No Title of Nobility shall be granted by the United States: And no Person holding any Office of Profit or Trust under them, shall, without the Consent of the Congress, accept of any present, Emolument, Office, or Title, of any kind whatever, from any King, Prince, or foreign State.

Section 10

Restrictions on States' Powers

1 No State shall enter into any Treaty, Alliance, or Confederation; grant Letters of Marque and Reprisal; coin Money; emit Bills of Credit; make any Thing but gold and silver Coin a Tender in Payment of Debts; pass any Bill of Attainder, ex post facto Law, or Law impairing the Obligation of Contracts, or grant any Title of Nobility.

2 No State shall, without the Consent of the Congress, lay any Imposts or Duties on Imports or Exports, except what may be absolutely necessary for executing its inspection Laws: and the net Produce of all Duties and Imposts, laid by any State on Imports or Exports, shall be for the Use of the Treasury of the United States; and all such Laws shall be subject to the Revision and Control of the Congress.

3 No State shall, without the Consent of Congress, lay any Duty of Tonnage, keep Troops, or Ships of War in time of Peace, enter into any Agreement or Compact with another State, or with a foreign Power, or engage in War, unless actually invaded, or in such imminent Danger as will not admit of delay.

ARTICLE II

THE EXECUTIVE BRANCH

Section 1

President and Vice President: Election, Qualifications, and Oath

1 The executive Power shall be vested in a President of the United States of America. He shall hold his Office during the term of four Years, and, together with the Vice President, chosen for the same Term, be elected, as follows.

2 Each State shall appoint, in such Manner as the Legislature thereof may direct, a Number of Electors, equal to the whole Number of Senators and Representatives to which the State may be entitled

* *Changed by the Sixteenth Amendment*

in the Congress: but no Senator or Representative, or Person holding an Office of Trust or Profit under the United States, shall be appointed an Elector.

3 [The Electors shall meet in their respective states, and vote by Ballot for two Persons, of whom one at least shall not be an Inhabitant of the same State with themselves. And they shall make a List of all the Persons voted for, and of the Number of Votes for each; which List they shall sign and certify, and transmit sealed to the Seat of the Government of the United States, directed to the President of the Senate. The President of the Senate shall, in the Presence of the Senate and House of Representatives, open all the Certificates, and the Votes shall then be counted. The Person having the greatest Number of Votes shall be the President, if such Number be a Majority of the whole Number of Electors appointed; and if there be more than one who have such Majority, and have an equal Number of Votes, then the House of Representatives shall immediately choose by Ballot one of them for President; and if no Person have a Majority, then from the five highest on the List the said House shall in like manner choose the President. But in choosing the President, the Votes shall be taken by States, the Representation from each State having one Vote; A quorum for this Purpose shall consist of a Member or Members from two thirds of the States, and a Majority of all the States shall be necessary to a Choice. In every Case, after the Choice of the President, the Person having the greatest Number of Votes of the Electors shall be the Vice President. But if there should remain two or more who have equal Votes, the Senate shall choose from them by Ballot the Vice President.]**

4 The Congress may determine the Time of choosing the Electors, and the day on which they shall give their Votes; which Day shall be the same throughout the United States.

5 No Person except a natural born Citizen, or a Citizen of the United States at the time of the Adoption of this Constitution, shall be eligible to the Office of the President; neither shall any person be eligible to that Office who shall not have attained to the Age of thirty five Years, and been fourteen Years a Resident within the United States.

6 [In Case of the Removal of the President from Office, or of his Death, Resignation, or Inability to discharge the Powers and Duties of the said Office, the Same shall devolve on the Vice President, and the Congress may by Law provide for the Case of Removal Death, Resignation or Inability, both of the President and Vice President, declaring what Officer shall then act as President, and such Officer shall act accordingly, until the Disability be removed, or a President shall be elected.]***

7 The President shall, at stated Times, receive for his Services, a Compensation, which shall neither be increased nor diminished during the Period for which he shall have been elected, and he shall not receive within that Period any other Emolument from the United States, or any of them.

8 Before he enter the Execution of his Office, he shall take the following Oath or Affirmation:—"I do solemnly swear (or affirm) that I will faithfully execute the Office of President of the United States, and will to the best of my Ability, preserve, protect, and defend the Constitution of the United States."

Section 2

Powers of the President

1 The President shall be Commander in Chief of the Army and Navy of the United States, and of the Militia of the several States, when called into the actual Service of the United States; he may require the Opinion, in writing, of the principal Officer in each of the executive Departments, upon any Subject relating to the Duties of their respective Offices, and he shall have Power to grant Reprieves and Pardons for Offenses against the United States, except in Cases of Impeachment.

2 He shall have Power, by and with the Advice and Consent of the Senate, to make Treaties, provided two thirds of the Senators present concur; and he shall nominate, and by and with the Advice and Consent of the Senate, shall appoint Ambassadors, other public Ministers and Consuls, Judges of the supreme Court, and all other Officers of the United States, whose Appointments are not herein otherwise provided for, and which shall be established by Law: but the Congress may by Law vest the Appointment of such inferior Officers, as they think proper, in the President alone, in the Courts of Law, or in the Heads of Departments.

** *Changed by the Twelfth Amendment*

*** *Changed by the Twenty-fifth Amendment*

3 The President shall have Power to fill up all Vacancies that may happen during the Recess of the Senate, by granting Commissions which shall expire at the End of their next Session.

Section 3

Duties of the President

He shall from time to time give to the Congress Information of the State of the Union, and recommend to their Consideration such Measures as he shall judge necessary and expedient; he may, on extraordinary Occasions, convene both Houses, or either of them, and in Case of Disagreement between them, with Respect to the Time of Adjournment, he may adjourn them to such Time as he shall think proper; he shall receive Ambassadors and other public Ministers; he shall take Care that the Laws be faithfully executed, and shall Commission all the Officers of the United States.

Section 4

Impeachment and Removal from Office for Crimes

The President, Vice President and all civil Officers of the United States, shall be removed from Office on Impeachment for, and Conviction of, Treason, Bribery, or other high Crimes and Misdemeanors.

ARTICLE III

THE JUDICIAL BRANCH

Section 1

Federal Courts, Tenure of Office

The judicial Power of the United States, shall be vested in one supreme Court, and in such inferior Courts as the Congress may from time to time ordain and establish. The Judges, both of the supreme and inferior Courts, shall hold their Offices during good Behavior, and shall, at stated Times, receive for their Services a Compensation, which shall not be diminished during their Continuance in Office.

Section 2

Jurisdiction of Federal Courts

1 The judicial Power shall extend to all Cases, in Law and Equity, arising under this Constitution, the Laws of the United States, and Treaties made, or which shall be made, under their Authority;—to all Cases affecting Ambassadors, other public Ministers and Consuls;—to all Cases of admiralty and maritime Jurisdiction;—to Controversies to which the United States shall be a Party;—to Controversies between two or more States; [between a State and Citizens of another State;]* between Citizens of different States;—between Citizens of the same State claiming Lands under Grants of different States;—[and between a State, or the Citizens thereof, and foreign States, Citizens or Subjects.]*

2 In all Cases affecting Ambassadors, other public Ministers and Consuls, and those in which a State shall be Party, the supreme Court shall have original Jurisdiction. In all the other Cases before mentioned, the supreme Court shall have appellate Jurisdiction, both as to Law and Fact, with such Exceptions, and under such Regulations as the Congress shall make.

3 The Trial of all Crimes, except in Cases of Impeach-ment, shall be by Jury; and such Trial shall be held in the State where said Crimes shall have been committed; but when not committed within any State, the Trial shall be at such Place or Places as the Congress may by Law have directed.

Section 3

Treason: Conviction Of and Punishment For

1 Treason against the United States shall consist only in levying War against them, or in adhering to their Enemies, giving them Aid and Comfort. No Person shall be convicted of Treason unless on the Testimony of two Witnesses to the same overt Act, or on Confession in open Court.

2 The Congress shall have Power to declare the Punishment of Treason, but no Attainder of Treason shall work Corruption of Blood, or Forfeiture except during the Life of the Person attainted.

ARTICLE IV

RELATIONS AMONG THE STATES

Section 1

Full Faith and Credit

Full Faith and Credit shall be given in each State to the public Acts, Records, and judicial Proceedings of every other State; And the Congress may by general Laws prescribe the manner in which such Acts, Records and Proceedings shall be proved, and the Effect thereof.

* *Changed by the Eleventh Amendment*

Section 2

Rights of State Citizens; Right of Extradition

1 The Citizens of each State shall be entitled to all Privileges and Immunities of Citizens in the several States.

2 A Person charged in any State with Treason, Felony, or other Crime, who shall flee from Justice, and be found in another State, shall on Demand of the executive Authority of the State from which he fled, be delivered up, to be removed to the State having Jurisdiction of the Crime.

3 [No person held to Service or Labour in one State, under the Laws thereof, escaping into another, shall, in Consequence of any Law or Regulation therein, be discharged from such Service or Labour, but shall be delivered up on Claim of the Party to whom such Service or Labour may be due.]**

Section 3

Admission of New States

1 New States may be admitted by the Congress into this Union; but no new State shall be formed or erected within the Jurisdiction of any other State; nor any State be formed by the Junction of two or more States, or parts of States, without the Consent of the Legislatures of the States concerned as well as of the Congress.

2 The Congress shall have Power to dispose of and make all needful Rules and Regulations respecting the territory or other Property belonging to the United States; and nothing in this Constitution shall be so construed as to Prejudice any Claims of the United States, or of any particular State.

Section 4

Republican Government Guaranteed

The United States shall guarantee to every State in this Union a Republican Form of Government, and shall protect each of them against Invasion; and on Application of the Legislature, or of the Executive (when the Legislature cannot be convened) against domestic Violence.

ARTICLE V

AMENDMENT PROCEDURES

The Congress, whenever two thirds of both Houses shall deem it necessary, shall propose Amendments to this Constitution, or, on the Application of the Legislatures of two thirds of the several States, shall call a Convention for proposing Amendments, which, in either Case, shall be valid to all Intents and Purposes, as Part of this Constitution, when ratified by the Legislatures of three fourths of the several States, or by Conventions in three fourths thereof, as the one or the other Mode of Ratification may be proposed by the Congress; Provided that no Amendment which may be made prior to the Year One thousand eight hundred and eight shall in any Manner affect the first and fourth Clauses in the Ninth Section of the first Article; and that no State, without its Consent, shall be deprived of its equal Suffrage in the Senate.

ARTICLE VI

SUPREMACY OF THE CONSTITUTION AND FEDERAL LAWS

1 All debts contracted and Engagements entered into, before the Adoption of this Constitution, shall be as valid against the United States under this Constitution, as under the Confederation.

2 This Constitution, and the Laws of the United States which shall be made in Pursuance thereof; and all Treaties made, or which shall be made, under the Authority of the United States, shall be the supreme Law of the Land; and the Judges in every State shall be bound thereby, any Thing in the Constitution or Laws of any State to the Contrary notwithstanding.

3 The Senators and Representatives before mentioned, and the Members of the several State Legislatures, and all executive and judicial Officers, both of the United States and of the several States, shall be bound by Oath or Affirmation, to support this Constitution; but no religious Test shall ever be required as a Qualification to any Office or public Trust under the United States.

ARTICLE VII RATIFICATION

The Ratification of the Conventions of nine States, shall be sufficient for the Establishment of this Constitution between the States so ratifying the Same.

Done in Convention by the unanimous consent of the States present the seventeenth day of September in the year of our Lord one thousand seven hundred and eighty seven and of the Independence of the United States of America the Twelfth. In witness whereof we have hereunto subscribed our Names,

** *Changed by the Thirteenth Amendment*

President and deputy from Virginia
George Washington

New-Hampshire
John Langdon
Nicholas Gilman

Massachusetts
Nathaniel Gorham
Rufus King

Connecticut
William Samuel Johnson
Roger Sherman

New York
Alexander Hamilton

New Jersey
William Livingston
David Brearley
William Paterson
Jonathan Dayton

Pennsylvania
Benjamin Franklin
Thomas Mifflin
Robert Morris
George Clymer
Thomas Fitzsimons
Jared Ingersoll
James Wilson
Gouverneur Morris

Delaware
George Read
Gunning Bedford, Jr.
John Dickinson
Richard Bassett
Jacob Broom

Maryland
James McHenry
Daniel of St. Tho. Jenifer
Daniel Carroll

Virginia
John Blair
James Madison, Jr.

North Carolina
William Blount
Richard Dobbs Spaight
Hugh Williamson

South Carolina
John Rutledge
Charles Cotesworth Pinckney
Charles Pinckney
Pierce Butler

Georgia
William Few
Abraham Baldwin

Attest:
William Jackson, Secretary

AMENDMENTS TO THE CONSTITUTION OF THE UNITED STATES OF AMERICA

The first ten amendments to the U.S. Constitution are known as the Bill of Rights. The Bill of Rights lists many basic rights that the federal government may not interfere with and must protect. Nearly all these rights are now also protected from violation by state governments. Subsequent amendments were adopted shortly afterward, beginning with the Eleventh Amendment in 1795. The Twenty-seventh Amendment is the most recent to be ratified. It became a part of the Consitution in 1992.

AMENDMENT I

Congress shall make no law respecting an establishment of religion, or prohibiting the free exercise thereof; or abridging the freedom of speech, or of the press; or the right of the people peaceably to assemble, and to petition the Government for a redress of grievances.

AMENDMENT II

A well regulated Militia, being necessary to the security of a free State, the right of the people to keep and bear Arms, shall not be infringed.

AMENDMENT III

No Soldier shall, in time of peace be quartered in any house, without the consent of the Owner, nor in time of war, but in a manner to be prescribed by law.

AMENDMENT IV

The right of the people to be secure in their persons, houses, papers, and effects, against unreasonable searches and seizures, shall not be violated, and no Warrants shall issue, but upon probable cause, supported by Oath or affirmation, and particularly describing the place to be searched, and the persons or things to be seized.

AMENDMENT V

No person shall be held to answer for a capital, or otherwise infamous crime, unless on a presentment or indictment of a Grand Jury, except in cases arising in the land or naval forces, or in the Militia, when in actual service in time of War or public danger; nor shall any person be subject for the same offence to be twice put in jeopardy of life or limb; nor shall be compelled in any criminal case to be a witness against himself, nor be deprived of life, liberty, or property, without due process of law; nor shall private property be taken for public use, without just compensation.

AMENDMENT VI

In all criminal prosecutions, the accused shall enjoy the right to a speedy and public trial, by an impartial jury of the State and district wherein the crime shall have been committed, which district shall have been previously ascertained by law, and to be informed of the nature and cause of the accusation; to be confronted with the witnesses against him; to have compulsory process for obtaining witnesses in his favor, and to have the Assistance of Counsel for his defence.

AMENDMENT VII

In Suits at common law, where the value in controversy shall exceed twenty dollars, the right of trial by jury shall be preserved, and no fact tried by a jury, shall be otherwise re-examined in any Court of the United States, than according to the rules of the common law.

AMENDMENT VIII

Excessive bail shall not be required, nor excessive fines imposed, nor cruel and unusual punishments inflicted.

AMENDMENT IX

The enumeration in the Constitution, of certain rights, shall not be construed to deny or disparage others retained by the people.

AMENDMENT X

The powers not delegated to the United States by the Constitution, nor prohibited by it to the States, are reserved to the States respectively, or to the people. [The first ten amendments were ratified December 15, 1791.]

AMENDMENT XI

The Judicial power of the United States shall not be construed to extend to any suit in law or equity, commenced or prosecuted against one of the United States by Citizens of another State, or by Citizens or Subjects of any Foreign State. [Ratified February 1795.]

AMENDMENT XII

The Electors shall meet in their respective states and vote by ballot for President and Vice-President, one of whom, at least, shall not be an inhabitant of the same state with themselves; they shall name in their ballots the person voted for as President, and in distinct ballots the person voted for as Vice-President, and they shall make distinct lists of all persons voted for as President, and of all persons voted for as Vice-President, and of the number of votes for each, which lists they shall sign and certify, and transmit sealed to the seat of the government of the United States, directed to the President of the Senate;—the President of the Senate shall, in the presence of the Senate and House of Representatives, open all the certificates and the votes shall then be counted;—The person having the greatest number of votes for President, shall be the President, if such number be a majority of the whole number of Electors appointed; and if no person have such majority, then from the persons having the highest numbers not exceeding three on the list of those voted for as President, the House of Representatives shall choose immediately by ballot, the President. But in choosing the President, the votes shall be taken by states, the representation from each state having one vote; a quorum for this purpose shall consist of a member or members from two-thirds of the states, and a majority of all the states shall be necessary to a choice. [And if the House of Representatives shall not choose a President whenever the right of choice shall devolve upon them, before the fourth day of March next following, then the Vice-President shall act as President, as in the case of the death or other constitutional disability of the President .—]* The person having the greatest number of votes as Vice-President, shall be the Vice-President, if such number be a majority of the whole number of Electors appointed, and if no person have a majority, then from the two highest numbers on the list, the Senate shall choose the Vice-President; a quorum for the purpose shall consist of two-thirds of the whole number of Senators, and a majority of the whole number shall be necessary to a choice. But no person constitutionally ineligible to the office of President shall be eligible to that of Vice-President of the United States. [Ratified June 1804.]

AMENDMENT XIII

Section 1

Neither slavery nor involuntary servitude, except as a punishment for crime whereof the party shall have been duly convicted, shall exist within the United States, or any place subject to their jurisdiction.

Section 2

Congress shall have power to enforce this article by appropriate legislation. [Ratified December 1865.]

AMENDMENT XIV

Section 1

All persons born or naturalized in the United States and subject to the jurisdiction thereof, are citizens of the United States, and of the State wherein they reside. No State shall make or enforce any law which shall abridge the privileges or immunities of citizens of the United States; nor shall any State deprive any person of life, liberty, or property, without due process of law; nor deny to any person within its jurisdiction the equal protection of the laws.

Section 2

Representatives shall be apportioned among the several States according to their respective numbers, counting the whole number of persons in each State, excluding Indians not taxed. But when the right to vote at any election for the choice of electors for President and Vice-President of the United States, Representatives in Congress, the Executive and Judicial officers of a State, or the members of the Legislature thereof, is denied to any of the male inhabitants of such State, being twenty-one years of age,** and citizens of the United States, or in any way abridged, except for participation in rebellion, or other crime, the basis of representation therein shall be reduced in the proportion which the number of such male citizens shall bear to the whole number of male citizens twenty-one years of age in such State.

* *Superseded by Section 3 of the Twentieth Amendment*

** *Changed by Section 1 of the Twenty-sixth Amendment*

Section 3

No person shall be a Senator or Representative in Congress, or elector of President and Vice-President, or hold any office, civil or military, under the United States, or under any State, who, having previously taken an oath, as a member of Congress, or as an officer of the United States, or as a member of any State legislature, or as an executive or judicial officer of any State, to support the Constitution of the United States, shall have engaged in insurrection or rebellion against the same, or given aid or comfort to the enemies thereof. But Congress may by a vote of two-thirds of each House, remove such disability.

Section 4

The validity of the public debt of the United States, authorized by law, including debts incurred for payment of pensions and bounties for services in suppressing insurrection or rebellion, shall not be questioned. But neither the United States nor any State shall assume or pay any debt or obligation incurred in aid of insurrection or rebellion against the United States, or any claim for the loss or emancipation of any slave; but all such debts, obligations and claims shall be held illegal and void.

Section 5

The Congress shall have the power to enforce, by appropriate legislation, the provisions of this article. [Ratified July 1868.]

AMENDMENT XV

Section 1

The right of citizens of the United States to vote shall not be denied or abridged by the United States or by any State on account of race, color, or previous condition of servitude.

Section 2

The Congress shall have the power to enforce this article by appropriate legislation. [Ratified February 1870.]

AMENDMENT XVI

The Congress shall have power to lay and collect taxes on incomes, from whatever source derived, without apportionment among the several States, and without regard to any census or enumeration. [Ratified February 1913.]

AMENDMENT XVII

The Senate of the United States shall be composed of two Senators from each State, elected by the people thereof, for six years; and each Senator shall have one vote. The electors in each State shall have the qualifications requisite for electors of the most numerous branch of the State legislatures. When vacancies happen in the representation of any State in the Senate, the executive authority of such State shall issue writs of election to fill such vacancies: *Provided*, That the legislature of any State may empower the executive thereof to make temporary appointments until the people fill the vacancies by election as the legislature may direct. This amendment shall not be so construed as to affect the election or term of any Senator chosen before it becomes valid as part of the Constitution. [Ratified April 1913.]

AMENDMENT XVIII

Section 1

After one year from the ratification of this article the manufacture, sale, or transportation of intoxicating liquors within, the importation thereof into, or the exportation thereof from the United States and all territory subject to the jurisdiction thereof for beverage purposes is hereby prohibited.

Section 2

The Congress and the several States shall have concurrent power to enforce this article by appropriate legislation.

Section 3

This article shall be inoperative unless it shall have been ratified as an amendment to the Constitution by the legislatures of the several States, as provided in the Constitution, within seven years from the date of the submission hereof to the States by the Congress. [Ratified January 1919.]***

AMENDMENT XIX

The right of citizens of the United States to vote shall not be denied or abridged by the United States or by any State on account of sex. Congress shall have power to enforce this article by appropriate legislation. [Ratified August 1920.]

*** *Repealed by the Twenty-first Amendment*

AMENDMENT XX

Section 1

The terms of the President and the Vice President shall end at noon on the 20th day of January, and the terms of Senators and Representatives at noon on the 3rd day of January, of the years in which such terms would have ended if this article had not been ratified; and the terms of their successors shall then begin.

Section 2

The Congress shall assemble at least once in every year, and such meeting shall begin at noon on the 3rd day of January, unless they shall by law appoint a different day.

Section 3

If, at the time fixed for the beginning of the term of the President, the President elect shall have died, the Vice President elect shall become President. If a President shall not have been chosen before the time fixed for the beginning of his term, or if the President elect shall have failed to qualify, then the Vice President elect shall act as President until a President shall have qualified; and the Congress may by law provide for the case wherein neither a President elect nor a Vice President elect shall have qualified, declaring who shall then act as President, or the manner in which one who is to act shall be selected, and such person shall act accordingly until a President or Vice President shall have qualified.

Section 4

The Congress may by law provide for the case of the death of any of the persons from whom the House of Representatives may choose a President whenever the right of choice shall have devolved upon them, and for the case of the death of any of the persons from whom the Senate may choose a Vice President whenever the right of choice shall have devolved upon them.

Section 5

Sections 1 and 2 shall take effect on the 15th day of October following the ratification of this article.

Section 6

This article shall be inoperative unless it shall have been ratified as an amendment to the Constitution by the legislatures of three-fourths of the several States within seven years from the date of its submission. [Ratified January 1933.]

AMENDMENT XXI

Section 1

The eighteenth article of amendment to the Constitution of the United States is hereby repealed.

Section 2

The transportation or importation into any State, Territory, or Possession of the United States for delivery or use therein of intoxicating liquors, in violation of the laws thereof, is hereby prohibited.

Section 3

This article shall be inoperative unless it shall have been ratified as an amendment to the Constitution by conventions in the several States, as provided in the Constitution, within seven years from the date of the submission hereof to the States by the Congress. [Ratified December 1933.]

AMENDMENT XXII

Section 1

No person shall be elected to the office of the President more than twice, and no person who has held the office of President, or acted as President, for more than two years of a term to which some other person was elected President shall be elected to the office of the President more than once. But this Article shall not apply to any person holding the office of President when this Article was proposed by the Congress, and shall not prevent any person who may be holding the office of President, or acting as President, during the term within which this Article becomes operative from holding the office of President or acting as President during the remainder of such term.

Section 2

This article shall be inoperative unless it shall have been ratified as an amendment to the Constitution by the legislatures of three-fourths of the several States within seven years from the date of its submission to the States by the Congress. [Ratified February 1951.]

AMENDMENT XXIII

Section 1

The District constituting the seat of Government of the United States shall appoint in such manner as the Congress may direct: A number of electors of President and Vice President equal to the whole number of Senators and Representatives in Congress to which the District would be entitled if it were a State, but in no event more than the least populous State; they shall be in addition to those appointed by the States, but they shall be considered, for the purposes of the election of President and Vice President, to be electors appointed by a State; and they shall meet in the District and perform such duties as provided by the twelfth article of amendment.

Section 2

The Congress shall have power to enforce this article by appropriate legislation. [Ratified March 1961.]

AMENDMENT XXIV

Section 1

The right of citizens of the United States to vote in any primary or other election for President or Vice President, for electors for President or Vice President, or for Senator or Representative in Congress, shall not be denied or abridged by the United States or any State by reason of failure to pay any poll tax or other tax.

Section 2

The Congress shall have power to enforce this article by appropriate legislation. [Ratified January 1964.]

AMENDMENT XXV

Section 1

In case of the removal of the President from office or of his death or resignation, the Vice President shall become President.

Section 2

Whenever there is a vacancy in the office of the Vice President, the President shall nominate a Vice President who shall take office upon confirmation by a majority vote of both Houses of Congress.

Section 3

Whenever the President transmits to the President pro tempore of the Senate and the Speaker of the House of Representatives his written declaration that he is unable to discharge the powers and duties of his office, and until he transmits to them a written declaration to the contrary, such powers and duties shall be discharged by the Vice President as Acting President.

Section 4

Whenever the Vice President and a majority of either the principal officers of the executive departments or of such other body as Congress may by law provide, transmit to the President pro tempore of the Senate and the Speaker of the House of Representatives their written declaration that the President is unable to discharge the powers and duties of his office, the Vice President shall immediately assume the powers and duties of the office as Acting President.

Thereafter, when the President transmits to the President pro tempore of the Senate and the Speaker of the House of Representatives his written declaration that no inability exists, he shall resume the powers and duties of his office unless the Vice President and a majority of either the principal office of the executive department or of such other body as Congress may by law provide, transmit within four days to the President pro tempore of the Senate and the Speaker of the House of Representatives their written declaration that the President is unable to discharge the powers and duties of his office. Thereupon Congress shall decide the issue, assembling within forty-eight hours for that purpose if not in session. If the Congress, within twenty-one days after receipt of the latter written declaration, or, if Congress is not in session, within twenty-one days after Congress is required to assemble, determines by two-thirds vote of both Houses that the President is unable to discharge the powers and duties of his office, the Vice President shall continue to discharge the same as Acting President; otherwise, the President shall resume the powers and duties of his office. [Ratified February 1967.]

AMENDMENT XXVI

Section 1

The right of citizens of the United States, who are eighteen years of age or older, to vote shall not be denied or abridged by the United States or by any State on account of age.

Section 2

The Congress shall have power to enforce this article by appropriate legislation. [Ratified July 1971.]

AMENDMENT XXVII

No law, varying the compensation for the services of the Senators or Representatives, shall take effect, until an election of Representatives shall have intervened. [Ratified May 1992.]

Glossary

abolish To put an end to.

amendment A change in or addition to a document.

American Revolution The war fought by the American colonists to gain their independence from Great Britain. It took place from 1775 to 1781.

appeal The bringing of a court case from a lower court to a higher court to be heard again.

Article I The part of the Constitution that describes the legislative branch of the government.

Article II The part of the Constitution that describes the executive branch of the government.

Article III The part of the Constitution that describes the judicial branch of the government.

Articles of Confederation The first constitution of the United States. It was adopted in 1781 and replaced in 1788 by our present Constitution.

balancing powers Balancing the powers of government means that no one branch is given so much power that it can completely control the other branches.

basic rights Fundamental rights, such as life, liberty, and property.

Bill of Rights The first ten amendments to the Constitution. It lists some basic rights of the people that the federal government may not interfere with and must protect.

bill A proposed law given to the legislature for approval.

boycott An act of protest, such as when people get together as a group and refuse to buy from or deal with a store or company.

cabinet A group made up of the heads of the departments of the executive branch. They advise the president.

checking power Limiting power.

checks and balances The sharing and balancing of power among different branches of government so no one branch can completely control the others.

Chief Justice The head of a court. The Chief Justice of the United States is head of the Supreme Court of the United States.

citizen A person who is a member of a nation.

civic virtue Putting the common good above individual interests.

Civil Rights Act of 1964 This law ended segregation in public places, including restaurants, movie theaters, and hotels. The law also said that employers could not unfairly discriminate against people because of their race, national origin, religion, or gender.

civil rights movement In the United States during the 1950s and 1960s, people organized to demand that the federal government protect the rights of African Americans and other minorities. People worked together to change unfair laws. They gave speeches, marched in the streets, and participated in boycotts.

Civil War The war between the Northern and Southern states. It took place from 1861 to 1865 and ended slavery in the United States.

Civil War Amendments The Thirteenth, Fourteenth, and Fifteenth Amendments to the Constitution passed after the Civil War. These amendments were intended to give former slaves the rights of citizens.

colony A settlement or territory ruled by another country.

commander in chief Highest leader of the military forces. In the United States, it is the president.

common defense Protection of the people from enemies.

common good The good of the community as a whole.

compromise A way to settle differences by each side giving up some of its claims or demands.

confederation A form of political organization in which states combine for specified purposes, such as defense. The United States was a confederation from 1776 to 1788.

conflict A struggle among differing ideas.

Congress The national legislature of the United States. Congress has two houses: the Senate and the House of Representatives.

consent of the governed The people agree to obey the laws and the government they create.

constitution A set of rules and laws that tells how a government is organized and run.

constitutional government A government in which the powers of the ruler or rulers are limited by a constitution. The rulers must obey the constitution.

Continental Congress The national legislature that governed the American colonies from 1774 until the adoption of the Articles of Confederation.

convention A formal assembly or meeting.

Declaration of Independence Statement that listed the basic principles of democratic government and gave reasons why the colonists wanted to free themselves from British rule. It was signed by the members of Congress on July 4, 1776.

delegate Used as a verb, it means to entrust someone to represent your interests. As a noun, it means the person chosen to act for you or represent you, usually at a convention or meeting.

defamation Purposely saying or writing false information about a person or group in a way that seriously injures their reputation.

democracy A form of government in which power is held by the people. The people exercise their power either directly or through elected representatives.

dictator A head of government who has unlimited power.

dictatorial government Government in which the rulers have unlimited power.

diplomacy The practice of managing relations between nations without use of warfare.

direct democracy This type of democracy means that the people themselves meet and make the laws that they decide are needed.

discrimination Unfair treatment of people because of such things as their race, religion, or gender.

diverse People of many different backgrounds.

domestic tranquility As used in the Preamble to the Constitution, this phrase means a peaceful situation within our country.

due process of law The requirement that procedures used by government in gathering information and making decisions be reasonable and fair.

Electoral College The group of presidential electors who cast the official votes for president and vice president after a presidential election. Each state has a number of electors equal to the total of its members in the Senate and House of Representatives.

enforce To make people obey the law.

equal protection clause The part of the Fourteenth Amendment that has been used to prevent states from being unfair to citizens because of their race or gender. It prohibits laws that unreasonably and unfairly favor some groups over others.

equal protection of the laws Treating all individuals or groups of people equally under the law, unless there is a good and fair reason for not doing so.

establishment clause The part of the First Amendment that says the government cannot set up an official religion.

executive branch The branch of government that carries out the laws made by the legislative branch.

executive power The authority to carry out and enforce the law.

expression To make known your thoughts and feelings.

federal courts The courts of the national government. They deal with problems between states, with the Constitution, and with laws made by Congress.

federal government Another name for our national government.

federal system A form of government in which power is divided between a central government and state and local governments.

Fifth Amendment It states that no person shall have their life, liberty, or property taken away by the federal government without due process of law. This amendment protects your right to be treated fairly by the federal government.

First Continental Congress The body of colonial delegates who convened to represent the interests of the colonists and protest British rule. The First Continental Congress met in 1774 and drafted a Declaration of Rights.

Founders The people who were important in the establishment of the United States.

Fourteenth Amendment It states that no person shall have their life, liberty, or property taken away by state or local governments without due process of law. This amendment protects your right to be treated fairly by your state and local governments. It also defines a citizen as anyone born or naturalized in the United States. It was one of the Civil War amendments.

Framers The delegates to the Philadelphia Convention of 1787.

free exercise clause The part of the First Amendment that says the government shall not stop you from holding any religious beliefs you choose. The government may not unfairly or unreasonably limit your right to practice any religious beliefs you wish.

freedom of assembly The right to meet with others to discuss your beliefs, ideas, or feelings.

freedom of belief or conscience The government may not force you to believe in something if you do not wish to do so.

freedom of expression The right to make known such things as your beliefs and opinions by means that are protected by the First Amendment.

freedom to petition The right to ask your government to correct things that you think are wrong or to do things you believe are needed.

freedom of the press The right to read and write whatever you wish, as well as the right to publish your ideas without government interference.

freedom of religion The right to hold whatever religious beliefs you wish and the right to practice your beliefs without unfair or unreasonable interference from the government.

fugitive slave clause The part of the Constitution that stated that slaves who escaped must be returned to their owners.

general welfare The good of all the people.

government The organization through which political authority is exercised.

grandfather clause The law stated that a person could vote if his grandfather had been allowed to vote. It made it possible for white people who could not pass a literacy test to vote because their grandfathers had the right to vote. It also made it impossible for African Americans to vote because their grandfathers had not been allowed to vote.

Great Compromise The plan accepted at the Philadelphia Convention that called for Congress to have two houses. The Senate would have two senators from each state. The House of Representatives would have representatives from each state based on its population.

hearing A meeting in which citizens give their views to public officials.

higher law A set of laws that are superior to other laws. For example, the U.S. Constitution is a higher law than any federal or state law.

House of Representatives One of two houses of Congress. The number of representatives from each state is based on its population.

humanitarian To have compassion and show concern for the pain and suffering of others.

immigrant A person who leaves his or her native land to settle in another country.

impeach To accuse a public official of committing a crime while he or she is in office.

indentured servant A person who agreed to work for someone for a set period of time in return for the cost of coming to America.

independence Self-rule; not ruled by another country.

interests Those things that are to your advantage or benefit.

interpret To explain the meaning of something.

judicial branch The branch of government that interprets and applies the laws and settles disputes.

judicial power The authority to settle disagreements about laws. This includes the power to say what the laws mean.

judicial review The power of the courts to say that the Constitution does not allow the government to do something.

Judiciary Act of 1789 The law that established the federal court system below the Supreme Court.

justices Members of the Supreme Court.

law A bill that has been passed by the legislature and signed by the executive or passed over an executive veto.

legislative branch The branch of government that makes the laws.

legislative power The authority to make laws and rules.

liberty, right to The right to be free. Some examples of liberties are the rights to believe what you wish, to read what you want, to speak freely, and to travel wherever you want to go.

life, right to The right to live without fear of being injured or killed by others.

limits Restrictions or boundaries.

literacy tests Tests given to people to prove they are able to read and write. These tests were used in the South to keep African Americans from voting.

Loyalists Americans who supported Great Britain during the Revolution.

majority More than half.

national government The organization having political authority in a nation.

natural rights Such basic rights as those to life, liberty, and property.

naturalized citizen Someone who is born elsewhere but who passes a citizenship test on the Constitution and the history of the United States.

Nineteenth Amendment Added to the Constitution in 1920, it gave women the right to vote.

Northwest Ordinance An important law passed by Congress in 1787 under the Articles of Confederation. The law provided for settling the western lands and organizing new states.

participation Taking part in or sharing in the activities of a group or organization.

Patriots Those Americans who supported the war for independence against Great Britain.

persecute To cause suffering to a person or group because of such things as their beliefs, gender, or race.

petition A formal, written request.

Philadelphia Convention The meeting held in Philadelphia in 1787 at which the U.S. Constitution was written.

plantation A large farm usually found in the Southern states.

politics A process by which people with different opinions and interests reach decisions without the use of violence.

poll tax A tax that voters in many states had to pay before they could vote.

popular vote The actual votes cast by the

people during a presidential election, rather than the votes cast by members of the Electoral College.

population The number of people living in an area.

Preamble The introduction to the Constitution. It states that the people establish the government and lists the purposes of the government.

press Newspapers, magazines, and other news media. Also, the reporters and people who produce them.

principle A rule or standard of behavior.

procedures The methods or steps taken to accomplish something.

property, right to The right to own things. Your labor or work is also your property.

ratification The formal approval of the Constitution by the states.

ratifying conventions Meetings held in the states to approve the Constitution.

represent To take the place of or to stand in for someone.

representatives People elected to act for others.

republic A country that has a government in which power is held by the people who elect representatives to manage the government for them.

republican government A government in which power is held by the people who elect representatives to run the government for the common good. The term does not refer to a political party.

resident alien A person who is not a citizen, but who lives legally in the United States. Resident aliens enjoy most of the rights of citizens. They have the same right to due process of law as citizens.

responsibility Duty or obligation.

Second Continental Congress The body of delegates representing the colonies that met in 1775 shortly after the start of the Revolutionary War. They organized the Continental Army and appointed a committee to draft the Declaration of Independence.

secretaries The heads of the departments in the executive branch who act as advisers to the president.

segregate To separate people in schools and other public places according to such things as their race.

self-sufficient Able to provide most of one's own needs.

Senate One house of Congress. Each state has two members in the Senate.

separation of powers The division of powers among the different branches of government. In the United States, powers are divided among the legislative, executive, and judicial branches.

slave A person whose human rights are denied and who is forced to work for another person.

slave trade The business of taking people from their homes in Africa and selling them in the colonies.

social contract An agreement among the people to set up a government and obey its laws.

speech, freedom of The right to talk about your beliefs, ideas, or feelings.

state of nature A situation in which there is no government, rules, or laws.

subject A person under the authority or rule of another.

supremacy clause The clause in the U.S. Constitution that explains that states cannot make laws that conflict with the U.S. Constitution or with the laws made by Congress.

Supreme Court The highest court in the United States.

testify Give information or evidence, as at a hearing or trial.

three-fifths clause The Framers' compromise about slavery that became part of the Constitution. It counted each slave as three-fifths of a person to determine how many representatives a state would have in Congress.

tolerant To be willing to let other people be different from yourself in such areas as religion, lifestyle, and political opinion.

trade The buying and selling of goods.

treaty An official agreement between two or more governments or rulers.

Twenty-fourth Amendment It states that the right to vote in a national election shall not be denied because a person fails to pay a poll tax or any other tax.

Twenty-sixth Amendment It gave citizens eighteen years of age or older the right to vote in all elections.

unconstitutional Not allowed by the U.S. Constitution; illegal.

United Nations An international organization created in 1945 to maintain peace and security for its members.

veto The power of the president to refuse to approve a bill passed by Congress.

Voting Rights Act The act passed in 1965 that further protected the right to vote for all U.S. citizens. It forced the states to obey the Constitution. It made it clear that the right to vote could not be denied because of a person's color or race.

witness A person who is called to give evidence before a court.

Index

A

B

C

LEGEND | Page numbers in bold indicate activities, debates, discussions, or exercises.

D

E

F

G

H

I

LEGEND | Page numbers in bold indicate activities, debates, discussions, or exercises.

J

K

L

M

N

O

P

R

LEGEND | Page numbers in bold indicate activities, debates, discussions, or exercises.

LEGEND | Page numbers in bold indicate activities, debates, discussions, or exercises.

Image Credits

Note: Many of the images listed below were licensed using Creative Commons licenses. These are listed with credits such as the following: CC BY-SA 3.0. Detailed information about this and other Creative Commons licenses can be found at www.creativecommons.org.

COVER

Washington Crossing the Delaware by Emanuel Leutze, 1851, Metropolitan Museum of Art, Gift of John Stewart Kennedy, 1897, Accession Number: 97.34.

FRONT MATTER

P. vi, Warren Burger, Supreme Court Historical Society.

INTRODUCTION

P. x, Rotunda for the Charters of Freedom, National Archives and Records Administration.

UNIT 1

P. 1, *Declaration of Independence* by John Trumbull, 1819, USCapitol/Wikimedia Commons.

LESSON 1

P. 3, *Vuë de Salem* by Balthasar Friedrich Leizelt, Prints and Photographs Division, Library of Congress, LC-DIG-ds-0720/Wikimedia Commons; 4, *Map of the United States in 1777* by Mapping Specialists/Center for Civic Education; 5, *The Treaty of Penn with the Indians* by Benjamin West, c. 1771, Pennsylvania Academy of Fine Arts/Wikimedia Commons; 6, *The Residence of David Twining* by Edward Hicks, 1845–48, Abby Aldrich Rockefeller Folk Art Collection/Wikimedia Commons; 7, *The Wiley Family* by William Williams, 1771, Smithsonian American Art Museum/Wikimedia Commons; 8, Richard Stein, Center for Civic Education; 9, *Abigail Adams* by Gilbert Stuart, c. 1810, National Gallery of Art/Wikimedia Commons.

LESSON 2

P. 11 *Writing the Declaration of Independence, 1776* by Jean Leon Gerome Ferris, Print and Photographs Division, Library of Congress, LC-USZC4-9904/Wikimedia Commons; 12, Harmony Day, DIAC images/Wikimedia Commons/CC BY 2.0; 13, Getty Images; 14, *John Locke, 1632 to 1704* by H. Garnier, Library of Congress, LC-USZ62-59655; 15–17, Richard Stein, Center for Civic Education.

LESSON 3

P. 19, *Cicero Denounces Catiline* by Cesare Maccari, 1889, Wikimedia Commons; 20, *Appius Claudius the Blind* by Cesare Maccari, 1882–1888, Wikimedia Commons; 21, Richard Stein, Center for Civic Education; 23, George Caleb Bingham, American, 1811–1879; *Stump Speaking*, 1853–54; oil on canvas; 42 1/2 x 58 inches; Saint Louis Art Museum, Gift of Bank of America 43:2001; 24, Campaign poster for William McKinley, c. 1895, Prints and Photographs Division, Library of Congress, LC-USZC4-1329; 26–27, Richard Stein, Center for Civic Education.

LESSON 4

P. 29, *Washington as Statesman at the Constitutional Convention* (cropped) by Junius Brutus Stearns, 1856, Virginia Museum of Fine Arts, CC-BY-NC; 30, 2009 Presidential Inauguration, Architect of the Capitol/Flickr; 32–37, Richard Stein, Center for Civic Education.

LESSON 5

P. 39, *The Rebels of '76*, c. 1860, Prints and Photographs Division, Library of Congress, LC-DIG-pga-03091; 40–43, Richard Stein, Center for Civic Education; 44, The Bostonian's Paying the Excise-man, or Tarring & Feathering, attributed to Philip Dawe, 1774, John Carter Brown Library, Brown University, Providence, Rhode Island/Wikimedia Commons; 45, Richard Stein, Center for Civic Education.

LESSON 6

P. 47, Old State House, Hartford, Connecticut, USA, by Charles Bulfinch, Daderot/Wikimedia Commons; 48–49, Richard Stein, Center for Civic Education; 51, King Charter 7, US Department of Education/Flickr/CC BY 2.0.

UNIT 2

P. 53, *The Foundation of American Government* by Henry Hintermeister, Prints and Photographs Division, Library of Congress, cph.3g02541.

LESSON 7

P. 55, *The First Continental Congress, 1774* by Allyn Cox, Architect of the Capitol, USCapitol/Flickr; 56, *Surrender of General Burgoyne* by John Trumbull, 1821, Architect of the Capitol/Wikimedia Commons; 57–61, Richard Stein, Center for Civic Education.

LESSON 8

P. 63, *Signing of the Constitution* by Howard Chandler Christy, 1940, Architect of the Capitol, USCapitol/Flickr; 64, *Board of Public Works Meeting* by Jay Baker, Maryland GovPics/Flickr/CC BY 2.0; 65, *The Constitutional Convention, 1787* by Allyn Cox, Architect of the Capitol, USCapitol/Flickr; 66 (top left), *George Washington* by Gilbert Stuart, 1797, Clark Art Institute/Wikimedia Commons; 66 (top right), *James Madison* by Gilbert Stuart, 1821, National Gallery of Art/Wikimedia Commons; 66, (bottom left), *Portrait of Benjamin Franklin* by Joseph Duplessis, c. 1785, National Portrait Gallery/Wikimedia Commons; 66 (bottom right), *Thomas Paine* by John Wesley Jarvis, c. 1806/1807, National Gallery of Art; 67 (left), *Thomas Jefferson* by Gilbert Stuart, c. 1821, National Gallery of Art; 67 (right), *Patrick Henry* by George Bagby Matthews, 1891, U.S. Senate Collection; 68–69, Richard Stein, Center for Civic Education.

LESSON 9

P. 71, U.S. President Barack Obama Delivers the 2011 State of the Union Address to a joint session of Congress, Lawrence Jackson, Executive Office of the President of the United States/Wikimedia Commons; 72–77, Richard Stein, Center for Civic Education.

LESSON 10

P. 79, *A Cotton Plantation on the Mississippi* by Nathaniel Currier and James Merritt Ives, 1884, Prints & Photographs Division, Library of Congress, LC-DIG-pga-00675; 81, *A Slave-coffle Passing the*

Capitol, c. 1876-81, Prints and Photographs Division, Library of Congress, LC-USZ62-2574; 83, Richard Stein, Center for Civic Education.

UNIT 3

P. 85, Visions of America, LLC/EyeWire Images.

LESSON 11

P. 87, Signed Copy of the Constitution of the United States, National Archives and Records Administration; 88, Old Nuclear Power Plant and New Wind Turbine, Jeanne Menjoulet/Flickr/CC BY 2.0; 89, Naturalization Ceremony Grand Canyon, Grand Canyon National Park/Flickr/CC BY 2.0; 90, Absentee Voting Night, U.S. Embassy photo by Vince Alongi, U.S. Embassy Montevideo, Embajada de los Estados Unidos en Uruguay/Flickr/Public Domain; 91, Four F-15 Eagle pilots, Tech. Sgt. Keith Brown/U.S. Air Force/Wikimedia Commons.

LESSON 12

P. 93, The Charters of Freedom in the Rotunda, U.S. National Archives/Flickr; 94, Photo by NEC Corporation of America with Creative Commons license CC BY 2.0; 96–97, Richard Stein, Center for Civic Education.

LESSON 13

P. 99, The western front of the United States Capitol, Architect of the Capitol/Flickr/Wikimedia Commons; 101, Richard Stein, Center for Civic Education; 102, Speaker of the House of Representatives Paul Ryan and the House Committee on Veterans' Affairs, June 23, 2017, Speaker Paul Ryan/Facebook; 103, Official photo of the 114th United States Congress, July 17, 2013, Speaker John Boehner/Flickr/Wikimedia Commons; 105–106, Richard Stein, Center for Civic Education.

LESSON 14

P. 109, White House North side (cropped), Tyler Loveless/Wikimedia Commons/CC BY-SA 3.0; 110, President Bush participates in a group photo with former presidents Gerald Ford, Richard Nixon, Ronald Reagan and Jimmy Carter in the replica of the Oval Office at the Dedication of the Ronald Reagan Presidential Library in Simi Valley, California, November 4, 1991, David Valdez/National Archives and Records Administration; 112, Governor O'Malley holds 2012 meeting of the electoral college by Tom Nappi at State House, Maryland GovPics/Flickr/CC BY 2.0; 113, Two days after the election, the President meets with President-elect Donald Trump, November 10, 2016, Official White House Photo by Pete Souza/Medium; 114–115, Richard Stein, Center for Civic Education.

LESSON 15

P. 117, U.S. Supreme Court Building, Architect of the Capitol, USCapitol/Flickr; 118, The Roberts Court, November 30, 2018, seated, from left to right, Justices Stephen G. Breyer and Clarence Thomas, Chief Justice John G. Roberts, Jr., and Justices Ruth Bader Ginsburg and Samuel A. Alito. Standing, from left to right: Justices Neil M. Gorsuch, Sonia Sotomayor, Elena Kagan, and Brett M. Kavanaugh, photograph by Fred Schilling, Supreme Court Curator's Office; 119–123, Richard Stein, Center for Civic Education.

LESSON 16

P. 125, Montana state capitol building by Geo. R. Mann, 1896, Prints and Photographs Division, Library of Congress, LC-DIG-pga-03345/Wikimedia Commons; 126, Restored Capitol Dome, U.S. Capitol/Flickr; 127, Richard Stein, Center for Civic Education; 128, Computer Science for All, U.S. Department of Education/Flickr/CC BY 2.0; 129, Richard Stein, Center for Civic Education; 130, Governor Wolf Signs Law Legalizing Ride-Sharing Statewide and a Bill Prohibiting State from Contracting with Businesses that Boycott Israel (cropped), Pennsylvania Governor Tom Wolf/Flickr/Wikimedia Commons/CC BY 2.0; 131, Art Opening (cropped), 2015, U.S. Department of Education/Flickr/CC BY 2.0.

UNIT 4

P. 133, *Embarkation of the Pilgrims* by Robert W. Weir, 1843, Architect of the Capitol/Flickr/Wikimedia Commons.

LESSON 17

P. 135, Presidential Scholars Dinner (cropped), U.S. Department of Education, Flickr/CC BY 2.0; 136, Signature, Garry Knight/Flickr/CC BY 2.0; 137, IMG_8016 (cropped and color/brightness adjustment), Photo by Charlie Furman, SumOfUs/Flickr/CC BY 2.0; 138, Maryland Governor Martin O'Malley Holds Press Conference on Ebola Preparedness by Jay Baker, Maryland GovPics, Flickr/CC BY 2.0; 139–143, Richard Stein, Center for Civic Education.

LESSON 18

P. 145, Lt. Jose Bautista Rojas offers the sacraments during a Catholic Mass aboard the Nimitz-class aircraft carrier USS John C. Stennis, U.S. Navy/Wikimedia Commons; 146, Jewish boy reading a Torah scroll at his Bar Mitzvah, Eli/Flickr/Wikimedia Commons/CC BY 2.0; 147, Richard Stein, Center for Civic Education; 148, A Congregation Sings God's Praises at the Freewell Missonary Baptist Church in Montgomery, Alabama, 2010, George F. Landegger Collection of Alabama Photographs in Carol M. Highsmith's America, Library of Congress, Prints and Photographs Division, LC-DIG-highsm-05802; 149 (left), Dr. Schreiber of San Augustine Giving a Typhoid Innoculation at a Rural School, San Augustine County, Texas, April 1943, John Vachon, Prints and Photographs Division, Library of Congress, LC-DIG-fsac-1a35422; 149 (right), Amish buggy on U.S. Route 30 in Lancaster County, Pennsylvania, Copyright Ad Meskens/Wikimedia Commons; 150, The School Day Opens with Prayer at Private School at the Farm Bureau Building, Pie Town, New Mexico, June 1940, Russell Lee, Prints and Photographs Division, Library of Congress, LC-USF34-036686-D; 151, Richard Stein, Center for Civic Education.

LESSON 19

P. 153, Civil Rights March on Washington, D.C., Rowland Scherman, U.S. Information Agency, National Archives and Records Administration/National Archives Identifier: 542010; 155, Army Gen. Ann E. Dunwoody meets New York police officers during a visit to the 9/11 Memorial in New York, Feb. 14, 2012, U.S. Army photo by Staff Sgt. Teddy Wade; 156, Man reading a newspaper with headline, "Presidential Proclamation, Slavery," which refers to the Jan. 1863 Emancipation Proclamation, H. L. Stephens, c. 1863, Prints and Photographs Division, Library of Congress, CaLC-USZC4-2442; 157, *Thurgood Marshall* by Thomas J. O'Halloran,

September 17, 1957, U.S. News & World Report Magazine Photograph Collection, Prints and Photographs Division, Library of Congress, LC-DIG-ppmsca-51775; 158, Participants, some carrying American flags, marching in the civil rights march from Selma to Montgomery, Alabama in 1965, Peter Pettus, Prints and Photographs Division, Library of Congress, LC-DIG-ppmsca-08102; 158, Civil Rights March on Washington, D.C., August 28, 1963, Rowland Scherman, National Archives and Records Administration, National Archives Identifier (NAID): 542015, restored by Adam Cuerden/Wikimedia Commons; 159, President Lyndon B. Johnson signs the 1964 Civil Rights Act, July 2, 1964, Cecil Stoughton, White House Press Office/Wikimedia Commons; 159, The 75th Air Base Wings's vice commander Col. David Lawrence (No. 51) and Wheelin' Wildcats player Aaron Summerill (No. 10) take the tip-off during the annual face off with Utah's semi-professional wheelchair basketball team, the Wheelin' Wildcats, Alex Lloyd, U.S. Air Force/Wikimedia Commons.

LESSON 20

P. 161, Richard Stein, Center for Civic Education; 162, Non Response Follow-Up in Houston, TX, Scott Dalton, U.S. Census Bureau; 163, Border Patrol agent reads the Miranda rights to a Mexican national arrested for transporting drugs, Gerald L. Nino, Customs and Border Protection, Department of Homeland Security/Wikimedia Commons; 164–165, Richard Stein, Center for Civic Education.

LESSON 21

P. 167, Youngest Parader in New York City Suffragist Parade, American Press Association/Prints and Photographs Division, Library of Congress/LC-USZC4-5585; 168, Governor Votes Early, Jay Baker, Maryland GovPics/Flickr/CC BY 2.0; 169, Richard Stein, Center for Civic Education; 170, Detail from *Lincoln's Second Inaugural, 1865*, by Allyn Cox, 1973–1974, Architect of the Capitol, USCapitol/Flickr; 171, Crowds surrounding the Reflecting Pool during the 1963 March on Washington, August 28, 1963, Warren K. Leffler, Prints and Photographs Division, Library of Congress, LC-U9-10363-5/Wikimedia Commons; 172, Elizabeth Cady Stanton, seated, and Susan B. Anthony, standing, three-quarter length portrait, c. 1880–1902, Prints and Photographs Division, Library of Congress, LC-USZ61-791; 173, 2005 Powwow, Katherine Fogden, Smithsonian Institution/Flickr/Wikimedia Commons.

UNIT 5

P. 175, Hall of the Charters of Freedom at the National Archives, Washington, D.C., Photographs in the Carol M. Highsmith Archive, Library of Congress, Prints and Photographs Division, LC-DIG-highsm-15714.

LESSON 22

P. 177, Secretary Tillerson Chairs a UN Security Council Meeting on Denuclearization of the DPRK, April 28, 2017, U.S. Department of State/Flickr; 178, U.S. Secretary of State John Kerry speaks with Astronaut Scott Kelly and Cosmonaut Mikhail Kornienko, who have been back on Earth for about three weeks since completing one year in space aboard the International Space Station, in Moscow, Russia, on March 24, 2016, U.S. State Department/Flickr; 179, IMO 9117325 Energy Ranger, Golden Gate Bridge, San Francisco, California, Prayitno/Flickr/CC BY 2.0;

180, Richard Stein, Center for Civic Education; 182, *Washington and Lafayette at Mount Vernon, 1784 (The Home of Washington after the War)* by Thomas Prichard Rossiter and Louis Remy Mignot, 1859, The Metropolitan Museum of Art; 183, Berlin, Germany, In November 1989, East German students sit atop the Berlin Wall at the Brandenburg Gate in front of border guards, University of Minnesota Institute of Advanced Studies/National Guard.

LESSON 23

P. 185, Chicago Immigration Protest May 1, 2006 (cropped), Joseph Voves, Flickr/CC BY 2.0; 186, Deputy Secretary Christopher Lu gives remarks to a Naturalization Ceremony of 500 new America citizens, at Oakton High School Vienna, VA, December 22, 2015 (cropped), U.S. Department of Labor, Shawn T, Moore, Flickr/Wikimedia Commons/CC BY 2.0; 187, Art Opening (cropped), U.S. Department of Education, Flickr/CC BY 2.0; 188, Recreation Host a Youth Forum, Montgomery County, MD, Flickr/Public Domain; 189, Rosary Prayer Service (cropped and lightened), Maryland GovPics, Flickr/CC BY 2.0; 190, Cassie Dorman, 18, in the black jacket, and Samantha Peterson, 18, register to vote at the booth outside Defoe-Graham Residence Hall Tuesday, Sept. 25, 2012 in Columbia, Mo, KOMUnews, Flickr/CC BY 2.0.

LESSON 24

P. 193, SAD Hortons Kids 114 (cropped), U.S. Department of Education, Flickr/CC BY 2.0; 194, Osan Girl Scouts honored Arbor Day and Earth Day by planting 200 moss flowers and 10 azalea bushes worth approximately $800 here, April 20, 2012, U.S. Air Force photo/Senior Airman Adam Grant; 196, Gas, Antti T. Nissinen, Flickr/CC BY 2.0; 197, Richard Stein, Center for Civic Education; 198, Center for Civic Education; 199, Richard Stein, Center for Civic Education.

REFERENCE

P. 201, *Portrait of Benjamin Franklin* by David Martin, 1767, White House/Wikimedia Commons.

STUDENTS!

CHECK OUT THE *WE THE PEOPLE* STUDENT RESOURCE CENTER

www.civiced.org/level1student

- **Lesson Purposes**
- **Lesson Objectives**
- **Terms to Know**
- **Biographies**
- **Primary Sources**
- **Media**

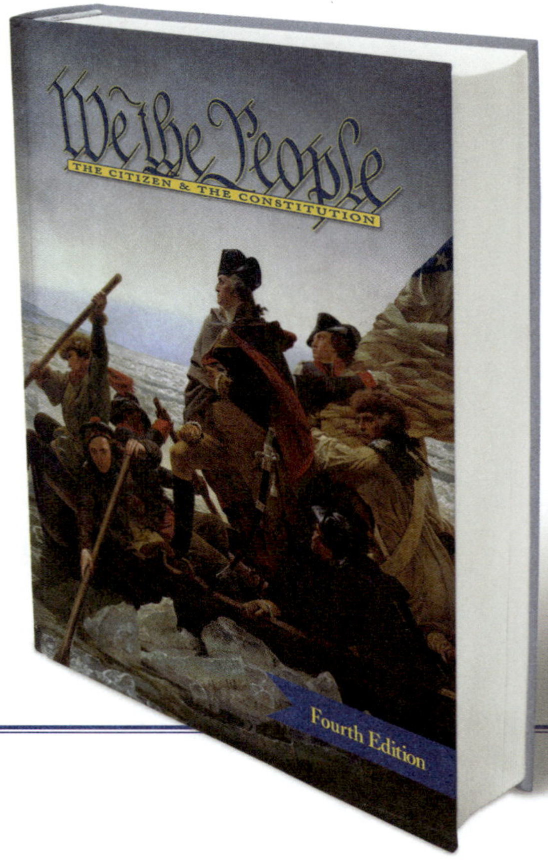